# DÜNGEONMEISTER™
## A DRINK MASTER'S GUIDE
### — THE —
## EXPANDED EDITION

# DÜNGEONMEISTER™
## A DRINK MASTER'S GUIDE
### THE
## EXPANDED EDITION

**RPG COCKTAILS AND MOCKTAILS TO SHAKE UP YOUR CAMPAIGN**

—⟨⋆⟩— JEF ALDRICH & JON TAYLOR —⟨⋆⟩—
CREATORS OF THE DÜNGEONMEISTER SERIES

**Adams Media**
New York  Amsterdam/Antwerp  London  Toronto  Sydney/Melbourne  New Delhi

Adams Media
An Imprint of Simon & Schuster, LLC
100 Technology Center Drive
Stoughton, MA 02072

For more than 100 years, Simon & Schuster has championed authors and the stories they create. By respecting the copyright of an author's intellectual property, you enable Simon & Schuster and the author to continue publishing exceptional books for years to come. We thank you for supporting the author's copyright by purchasing an authorized edition of this book.

No amount of this book may be reproduced or stored in any format, nor may it be uploaded to any website, database, language-learning model, or other repository, retrieval, or artificial intelligence system without express permission. All rights reserved. Inquiries may be directed to Simon & Schuster, 1230 Avenue of the Americas, New York, NY 10020 or permissions@simonandschuster.com.

Copyright © 2020, 2025 by
Simon & Schuster, LLC.

All rights reserved, including the right to reproduce this book or portions thereof in any form whatsoever. For information, address Adams Media Subsidiary Rights Department, 1230 Avenue of the Americas, New York, NY 10020.

This Adams Media hardcover edition
October 2025
First Adams Media hardcover edition
December 2020

ADAMS MEDIA and colophon are registered trademarks of Simon & Schuster, LLC.

Düngeonmeister is a trademark of Simon & Schuster, LLC.

Simon & Schuster strongly believes in freedom of expression and stands against censorship in all its forms. For more information, visit BooksBelong.com.

For information about special discounts for bulk purchases, please contact Simon & Schuster Special Sales at 1-866-506-1949 or business@simonandschuster.com.

The Simon & Schuster Speakers Bureau can bring authors to your live event. For more information or to book an event, contact the Simon & Schuster Speakers Bureau at 1-866-248-3049 or visit our website at www.simonspeakers.com.

Interior design by Kellie Emery
Interior images by Priscilla Yuen, Claudia Wolf, and Frank Rivera

Manufactured in the United States of America

10 9 8 7 6 5 4 3 2 1

Library of Congress Control Number: 2025940318

ISBN 978-1-5072-2449-6
ISBN 978-1-5072-2450-2 (ebook)

Many of the designations used by manufacturers and sellers to distinguish their products are claimed as trademarks. Where those designations appear in this book and Simon & Schuster, LLC, was aware of a trademark claim, the designations have been printed with initial capital letters.

Always follow safety and commonsense cooking protocols while using kitchen utensils, operating ovens and stoves, and handling uncooked food. If children are assisting in the preparation of any recipe, they should always be supervised by an adult.

Contains material adapted from the following title published by Adams Media, an Imprint of Simon & Schuster, LLC: *Düngeonmeister* by Jef Aldrich & Jon Taylor, copyright © 2020, ISBN 978-1-5072-1465-7.

# Contents

### Introduction / 11

### Tavern Basics / 13
Essential Spirits for Tavern Keeping / 14
How to Modify Your Recipes for Alcohol-Free Drinks / 16
Common On-Hand Mixers / 17
Basic Bar Tools You'll Need to Get Started / 20

### Chapter 1: Spirited Species / 21
Three Halflings in a Trench Coat / 22
Dark Elf / 25
Gnomish Gnightcap / 26
Dwarven Forge / 29
Aasimartini / 31
Half 'n' Half-Orc / 32
Sleep Immunity / 34
Tiefling's Breakfast / 35
Slippery Grippli / 37
Pixie Dust / 38

## Chapter 2: Class-y Drinks / 41

Barbarian Rage / 43

Bard's Songs / 44

Flavored Enemy / 46

Holy Water / 47

Necromancer / 49

Sneak Attack / 50

Stunning Smite / 51

Sweet and Sour-cerer / 52

Gnomish Illusionist / 55

Sword and Chambord / 56

## Chapter 3: Skilled Selections / 57

Healing Surge / 58

Escape Artist / 60

Point Blank Shot / 61

Seduction Roll / 63

Power Attack / 64

Royal Diplomacy / 65

Stealth Checks / 66

Turn Undead / 69

Sprite of Hand / 70

Twin Strikes / 72

## Chapter 4: Magic Mixers / 73

Acid Arrow / 75

Coors Light Wounds / 76

Elemental Plane of Fire / 77

Black Mana / 78

Green Mana / 81

Faerie Fire / 82

Hpnotiq Pattern / 83

Blue Mana / 84

Red Mana / 87

White Mana / 88

Magic Mistletoe / 91

Psionic Blasts / 92

Peanut Butter & Jellikinesis / 95

Goodberries / 96

## Chapter 5: Muddled Minions / 97

Gelatinous Cubes / 98

Giant Bee / 101

Goblin Grenades / 102

Illithid Substance / 104

1d3 Wandering Minstrels / 106

Kobold Fashioned / 107

Mermaid Lagoon / 109

Troll Slobber / 110

Wight Russian / 113

Gin and Skeletonic / 114

Rust Monster / 116

## Chapter 6: Immense Intoxicants / 117

The 666 Layers of the Abyss, Now with Coconut / 119

Breath Weapon / 120

Nature Goddess / 122

Claw Claw Snakebite / 123

Dragon the Beach / 125

Mai Tyrant / 126

Purple Worm / 128

Silver Dragon / 129

Release the Kraken / 131

Girallon and On / 132

## Chapter 7: Metagame Madness / 135

Düngeonmeister / 137

Horror Factor / 138

Fudge the Dice / 140

The Level Up / 141

The Natural 20 / 143

Never Split the Party Punch / 144

Session Zero / 146

The TPK / 147

Peek Behind the Screen / 149

## Chapter 8: Alcoholic Artifacts / 151

Treasure Type J / 152
Astral Diamond Juice / 153
Electrum Piece / 154
Magic Mirror / 156
Potion of Glibness / 157
Epic Upgrade / 159
Pool of Radiance / 160
Potion of Strength / 163
Golden Hoard / 164

## Chapter 9: Phantom Fluids / 167

Color Spray / 169
Hallucinatory Garden Terrain / 170
Black Magic Mirror / 171
SimulacRum Punch / 172
Banana Balhannoth / 175
Magic Mouth / 176
Coupe of Elvenkind / 178
Invisibilitea / 179
Ranch Water Weird / 181
Blur Berry / 182

## US/Metric Conversion Chart / 183

## Index / 185

# INTRODUCTION

Congratulations on finding *Düngeonmeister: The Expanded Edition*, a book helpful for any would-be adventuring barkeep, or Game Master! This celebrated guide to cocktail craft with a fantasy RPG twist has leveled up, becoming bigger and better than ever. We know that the best thing about role-playing is the way that it brings people together, especially when those people are adults with full schedules. So why not make your gatherings even more special and focused on the sense of community you've established with delightful and amusing beverages? Whether your nerdy night includes board gaming, movie watching, or just hanging out with friends, this expanded edition really helps take things up a notch.

With more than ninety different drink recipes, this expanded edition offers an assortment of flavors in various forms, including shots, single drinks, or even punch bowls. Throughout these pages, you'll find new content like a chapter of mocktails, a brand-new beverage in every older chapter, and a helpful guide on modifying recipes to be nonalcoholic. Plus, it's amazing what spellbinding recipes you'll come across throughout this new *Düngeonmeister*. Try to glimpse a Sprite of Hand or an elusive Peanut Butter & Jellikinesis, or if you're looking for something light, try an Invisibilitea mocktail or Hallucinatory Garden Terrain mocktail. Whatever your or your players' preference, there is something here to quench their desire: sweet and fruity tropical tiki drinks, sharp and bitter beverages to jolt the senses, and even things for those that just want to min-max their version of a good time.

For any novice barkeeps, there's a Tavern Basics section to let you know what tools and tricks you can use to make your best drinks.

Every recipe includes a complexity rating so you can divine how involved a drink will be. Not everyone has the time or energy to break out the blender or craft their own honey syrup when they want a beverage. The Complexity 1 recipes will require the ingredients for the drink and a cocktail shaker to mix them up. If you're questing for something more unique, the higher complexity drinks will see you brewing up your own teas and might require special ordering certain powders for mesmerizing special effects. For an additional dash of fun, however, most recipes come with humorous sidebars so even when you're not pouring one out, you can still find mirth and merriment as you're flipping through.

If you're searching for an immersive treat, try to plan ahead and match the drink to the adventure you're having! The chapters make this particularly easy. Each chapter is themed around a particular part of the RPG world, from species to artifacts to magic and more. Are the players currently making their way through a dragon's lair? Maybe mix up a Dragon the Beach or a Golden Hoard. Are they being chased by zombies? A nice Black Mana or Gin and Skeletonic will make them feel better (though they will still need to do *something* about those pesky undead).

Whatever your alcohol (or nonalcohol) preference, desired complexity, or thirst for adventure, you can easily use these recipes to make your adventuring party into partiers.

# TAVERN BASICS

It's only natural that epic quests begin in taverns. There's a sense of camaraderie; warmth from the hearth; simple, well-cooked meals; and, of course, copious tankards of fortifying alcohol. It's a rookie mistake to take these simple pleasures for granted, and if you're feeling like taking your game up to the next level of realistic verisimilitude, then why not set up your own pregame tavern? With our help, you'll be slinging characterful cocktails (or mocktails) and potent potions that help infuse a little more spirit (occasionally using more spirits) into your dungeon adventures.

In this section you'll find:

- The basic alcohols or zero-proof alternatives you need for the drinks in this book
- A list of mixers
- The essential bar tools to make drinks

With all this, you'll be ready to plunge right in (so to speak) to the drinks in the rest of the book. But what should your tavern include (besides plenty of adventurers and mysterious old men muttering to themselves in a corner)?

# Essential Spirits for Tavern Keeping

All fully-stocked bars begin with a collection of spirits that forms an important part of mixology. Perhaps while setting up a place for dwarves or half-orcs, one can get away with ales ranging from strong to unpleasant, but if plans stray toward entertaining other players at the tavern table, it's best to start with a collection of the classics. Otherwise, you'll find yourself in the unenviable position of trying to sling glasses of orange juice and sweet and sour mix to less than appreciative patrons and friends.

## Vodka

Vodka is invariably the most used spirit in the bar. It's the go-to for cocktail making, and you'll find it in most cocktail recipes. Distilled most commonly from grain or potato starch (but in reality can be made from nearly anything floral), vodka's claim to fame is a lack of flavor, meaning it can add a kick without adding a note.

## Gin

Gin, like vodka, is a distilled spirit, though instead of lacking flavor, it has many potential flavors. Gin is an exceptionally broad category of like spirits, which all feature juniper berry as a flavor note in common (and often not much else). In most recipes that call for gin, you can use any type you want—the exception being sloe gin. Sloe gin is flavored by a sour little blue fruit known as a blackthorn, which changes its flavor profile from other gins immensely, and also makes it the alcohol with the best flavor profile to steal for character names. Unless otherwise noted, recipes that call for gin can use any gin you have on hand. If the recipe calls for something more specific, we'll be sure to say so.

## Rum

Through the power of sugarcane (molasses or syrup), rum picks up deep, toasty sugar flavors. Beyond this, it can be difficult to ascribe any major catchall descriptions to rum, in no small part because few countries can agree on what rum even is! For our purposes, rum is generally either light (clear; also known as white or silver) or spiced (some variation of a darker gold or caramel). It is also the perfect libation to add authenticity to adventures set on the high seas. Just keep it away from the powder barrels, please.

## Tequila

Most of the major spirits can be made from a variety of source ingredients. Such is not the case with tequila, distilled from primarily blue agave, and made only in Mexico. This specificity lends tequila a collection of stereotypes, most of which are unearned. While cheap mass-produced tequilas can be harsh and unpleasant, there are also exceptional blends and distillations so fine and smooth they are best served straight for sipping.

## Whiskey

Much like gin, whiskey is so varied in tone, flavor, ingredients, and profile that it can be hard to know what sort to add to a drink. Speaking most generally, whiskey is a spirit made from fermenting grain mash, generally aged in wooden barrels or casks to develop maturity, color, and flavor. Ever wonder about the difference between whiskey and whisky? Us too. Someone probably answers that in a book somewhere.

# How to Modify Your Recipes for Alcohol-Free Drinks

It has never been easier to make a drink that can convey the experience and flavor of a cocktail without the booze! No longer are we shackled to having a soda with some grenadine in it (though a Shirley Temple is delicious, and we'll hear no argument against it). There are plenty of alternatives that can be used in place of standard spirits that are zero proof and the occasional ones that are still made through fermentation but have a negligible amount of alcohol in them, such as kombucha or The Pathfinder (an amaro substitute).

If a cocktail is relatively simple and only requires a single spirit with a handful of mixers, you can easily swap out the alcoholic ingredient with a nonalcoholic spirit. For instance, if making a standard gin and tonic, you would replace the gin with a zero-proof gin alternative. You'll find that certain spirit substitutes might end up tasting more or less convincing, so depending on personal taste, you might have to shop around to find one that suits the specific flavor profile you're looking for.

Some alternatives include Clean V or Strykk for vodka, Gnista Barreled Oak or Monday Zero for whiskey, Ritual or Petit Béret Natural Botanic for gin, Spiritless Jalisco 55 or CleanCo for tequila, and Sober Spirits or Fluère Spiced Cane for rum. Plus, the Escape Wise brand covers many types of liqueurs. There are lots of brands beyond these, as well, so pick your favorites!

When making a mocktail for someone who simply wants the *feel* of having a mixed drink without the alcohol, you can always just make the drink without the alcohol. If it lacks a bite, try subbing in a splash of nonalcoholic ginger beer, kombucha, or other powerful flavors. Use what works for your palate. Most, if not all, drinks can be made into mocktails, and with all the choices and substitutes available, you can find a wide variety of delicious options.

## Common On-Hand Mixers

Most of the simple mixers you'll want on hand for a tavern party are self-explanatory. Juices, milk, soft drinks, and the like require little explanation. We'd still provide one for each, but unlike RPG authors, we don't get paid by the word, so you figure out those mixers. Following is a guide to basic syrups that can be easily made at home, as well as a few of the more esoteric ingredients found in this book.

### Simple Syrup

This common mix-in couldn't be easier to get set up in your home bar tool kit. It's just equal parts granulated sugar and water, simmered and stirred until the sugar is dissolved, and then stored in the refrigerator until it's called for. That's it. That's the entire recipe. (For a cinnamon-flavored version, you can include a couple of cinnamon sticks.)

### Rosemary Syrup

This is a twist on the classic simple syrup. It's 4 cups water, 4 cups granulated sugar, and about 1 ounce of rosemary (2–4 sprigs). Once you have the appropriate amount of rosemary, you'll do everything the same as with the simple syrup recipe, throwing the rosemary in at the same time as the sugar. Super easy.

### Goodberry Syrup

Another twist on the original simple syrup. It's made up of 1 cup water, ¾ cup granulated sugar, and 1 cup frozen mixed berries. First, put everything in a saucepan over medium heat. Cook 4–5 minutes until simmering and the juices from the berries have come out. Then you'll do everything else the same as the basic simple syrup recipe—just strain the berries out at the end!

### Grape Jelly Simple Syrup

Instead of sugar, this one just takes ½ cup Concord grape jelly and ½ cup water. Then do everything the same as in the basic simple syrup recipe. What a yummy twist!

> **Complex Syrup**
>
> This exceptionally difficult to manufacture fluid is also famously challenging to imbibe and digest. No recipes in this book call for it, and we've never seen it required elsewhere. However, the existence of simple syrup suggests that complex syrup must exist, and it is therefore included for the sake of completion, as most nerdy things are.

### Honey Syrup

Honey can be difficult to utilize in cocktail construction, since it will harden in cold water and not mix well no matter how much you stir it. A shame, since honey can lend a variety of floral and earthy sweet flavors to cocktails. There's a solution though, quite literally.

Just combine 1 cup honey and ½ cup warm water in your squeeze bottle of choice and give the whole thing a good shake. This flavorful concoction will keep for weeks on the counter or in the refrigerator. It also works with flavored or hot honeys. You'll find a few recipes in this book that call for either honey syrup or spicy hot honey syrup.

## Sweet and Sour Mix

Yes, you can just buy this in stores. That said, you can also just get cocktails in bars, so let's apply that can-do spirit and make your own delicious sweet and sour mix for a variety of cocktails. It's easy! Just mix equal parts water, sugar, fresh lemon juice, and fresh lime juice. And if you already have simple syrup, just use one part of that instead of the water and sugar. Don't cook this one; just combine, mix, and store for later. Oh, and if you'd like margarita mix, keep the ratio, but don't put in the lemon juice. One part each sugar, water, and lime juice is all you need for classic marg-crafting.

## Citric Acid

There are dozens of household uses for this powdered acid product. It can be used for cleaning, as a foaming agent, and in cosmetics and pharmaceuticals. For the purposes of this book, we primarily use it for the chapter on how to chelate limescale off your hot water heater and associated fixtures. Just kidding! We use it in place of lemon juice in recipes that call for both sourness and clarity. It's readily available in stores and online.

## Luster Dust

A tiny amount of this goes a very long way. This is essentially superfine edible glitter that you can mix into drinks to give them a visible "magicky" shimmer effect. You've likely seen it already mixed with some drinks available in stores. It's easy to find in a variety of colors online and in the cake decorating aisle of grocery stores.

## Basic Bar Tools You'll Need to Get Started

You'll require a cocktail shaker for most of these cocktails. Bar spoons and measuring spoons or cups that show small ounce amounts would also be exceptionally useful. As for glassware, there is a dazzling, near-infinite array of types of glasses that you can use to serve libations in, from the humble highball to the swoopy Nick and Nora. You don't need to concern yourself too much with having the perfect glass set for every occasion, however, and can do quite well starting out with some shot glasses, martini glasses, and rocks glasses. In each recipe we've suggested the appropriate glass, but if you don't have it, no sweat. Just use what you've got on hand.

All right. Now you know the basics. Let's get mixing, people! Adventuring parties, in search of dragons, are getting thirsty.

# Chapter 1

## SPIRITED SPECIES

Constantly in search of dragons, adventuring parties are getting thirsty. Within this chapter, you'll discover beverages inspired by orcs, dwarves, elves, and similar denizens of dungeons and drinkeries. Choose wisely, as your selection will impact your attributes. (*Düngeonmeister: The Expanded Edition* uses thirteen unique and proprietary attributes but wholeheartedly believes that attributes should be up to the bartender, thus their obvious omission from all future recipes.)

# Three Halflings in a Trench Coat

**Complexity: 1**  **Yields 1 cocktail**

It is a well-known fact that there is little more terrifying or confusing than the combined might of three halflings in a trench coat coming right at you. In the same way, the three rums that find themselves hidden in a coat of sweetness and sour juices are a total powerhouse.

1 ounce light rum
1 ounce dark rum
1 ounce demerara rum
¾ ounce lime juice
¾ ounce white grapefruit juice
1 ounce honey syrup (see recipe in Tavern Basics)
2 ounces club soda
1 orange wheel
3 stemmed maraschino cherries

1. Fill a cocktail shaker with ice. Add rums, juices, and syrup.
2. Shake and strain into a Collins glass filled with ice. Top with club soda.
3. Skewer orange wheel. Garnish with skewered orange wheel and cherries.

> **DÜNGEONMEISTER TIP**
>
> Originally, there were only two halflings in a trench coat, and it was just so they could get into bars and restricted movies. It wasn't until an enterprising third joined in that the world knew the true power of a wobbly mass with six arms and a dapper fashion sense.

# Dark Elf

**Complexity: 1**  **Yields 1 cocktail**

Deep in the recesses of the underworld, the shadowy dark elves plot and conspire in the pitch-dark of the eternal night. Sitting around plotting in darkness isn't especially inspiring, so they often sit at fancy tables drinking exotic underworld cocktails made from secretive, maleficent ingredients. Since maleficent ingredients are often not dolphin-safe or free of GMOs, we've attempted to re-create the umbral nectars these elves enjoy using simple ingredients.

- 2 ounces light rum
- ¾ ounce peach schnapps
- 3 ounces cherry juice (as dark as possible)
- 2 teaspoons grenadine
- 2 stemmed and pitted fresh dark cherries (such as Bing or Sweetheart)
- 2 stemmed maraschino cherries

1. Fill a cocktail shaker with ice. Add rum, schnapps, cherry juice, and grenadine.

2. Shake and strain into a martini glass. Spear alternating fresh and maraschino cherries on a toothpick and add as garnish.

# Gnomish Gnightcap

**Complexity: 1**                                                    **Yields 1 cocktail**

Gnomes are gnown for having gnightcaps that are gnothing short of magnificent. Bitter, sweet, dry, and refreshing all at once, this drink is every bit as complex as any gnomish invention, but it's exceedingly easy to make.

*1 ounce London Dry gin*
*1 ounce Campari*
*1 ounce sweet vermouth*
*1 orange twist (peel)*

1. Fill a cocktail shaker with ice. Add all ingredients except orange twist.
2. Shake and strain into a highball glass filled with ice. Garnish with orange twist.

> **DÜNGEONMEISTER TIP**
>
> The tradition of ending an evening with a drink is attributed to Delbar Tippletinkler, a hero among the gnomish people. Originally, the drink had a sprinkle of dirt in it as well. Not on purpose. That's just what happens when you make all your drinks in a burrow.

# Dwarven Forge

**Complexity: 3**                                    **Yields 1 cocktail**

Dwarves are master craftsmen, known far and wide for their attention to detail, resistance to the heat of their mighty furnaces, and mastery over the blend of artistry and function. To pay proper homage to the stout axe-loving folk, this cocktail is a challenge to make and a reward to master. It's also on fire, so be extremely careful and follow all recommended safety instructions.

*For the Spiced Berry Coulis:*
12 ounces frozen berry blend
3 thyme sprigs
½ cup granulated sugar
½ cup water
2 drops red food coloring

*For the Cocktail:*
2 ounces spiced rum
1½ ounces Spiced Berry Coulis
¾ ounce lemon juice
2 teaspoons overproof rum

1. For the Spiced Berry Coulis: Combine all ingredients except food coloring in a medium saucepan.

2. Cook over medium heat to boiling, stirring until all sugar has dissolved and fruit has fully softened, roughly 8 minutes.

3. Remove mixture from the heat, transfer to a medium bowl, and refrigerate until cold, at least 1 hour.

4. Strain mixture through a sieve into a small storage bottle (a funnel may help here), then add food coloring for extra color. Stir to combine.

5. Refrigerate until ready to use.

6. For the Cocktail: Fill a cocktail shaker with ice. Add all ingredients except overproof rum.

7. Shake and strain into a coupe glass, leaving room at the top of the glass.

8. Slowly pour overproof rum over the back of a bar spoon into the glass to form a layer over top of cocktail (be careful not to fill the glass).

9. Light cocktail with a match and observe. Safety note: Do not move cocktail or consume cocktail while still lit. Do not attempt to blow out a flaming cocktail. To put out, smother the fire with a saucer or cocktail shaker. Do not allow the fire to "burn out," as alcohol fires can be invisible. Always ensure fire is safely out before consuming.

> **DÜNGEONMEISTER TIP**
>
> For maximum Dwarven Forge showiness, wait until this drink is lit and burning, then from a safe distance above the flames, sprinkle a pinch of cinnamon down from above. This will create beautiful forge sparks, which dwarves hold in high esteem (at beard's length, of course).

# Aasimartini

**Complexity: 1**                          **Yields 1 cocktail**

A cocktail as holy as drinking it can legally be outside of a church or temple, the Aasimartini distills divinity into a delightful package. While the Aasimar merely has an angel or two somewhere in the family tree, the Aasimartini delivers glory on high and a pleasant coffee aroma to boot.

*2 ounces Irish cream liqueur*
*1 ounce vodka*
*1 ounce brewed espresso*
*1 star fruit slice*

1. Place a martini glass in the freezer, allowing it to chill as you prepare the drink.
2. Fill a cocktail shaker with ice. Add all ingredients except fruit slice.
3. Shake and strain into chilled martini glass. Garnish with star fruit slice.

> **DÜNGEONMEISTER TIP**
>
> Several variations on this cocktail exist, from the Half-Celestial Templarita to the Deva & Coke, but we've elected to include the original, because that's the lawful good thing to do.

# Half 'n' Half-Orc

**Complexity: 1**                                **Yields 1 cocktail**

Half-orcs have a hard time fitting into society. They are rejected by their brutal orcish cousins and treated as dangerous criminals and monsters by their human relatives. There is, however, a fierce nobility to these folk, and those that do befriend them are rewarded, in this case by a refreshing blend of mint and cream that's a treat for just about everyone.

*1 ounce green crème de menthe*
*1 ounce crème de cacao*
*2 ounces half-and-half*

1. Place a martini glass in the freezer, allowing it to chill as you prepare the drink.

2. Fill a cocktail shaker with ice. Add all ingredients.

3. Stir gently with a bar spoon until cold, then strain into chilled martini glass.

> **DÜNGEONMEISTER TIP**
>
> The Half 'n' Half-Orc is best garnished with mint leaves, but dark chocolate shavings are a crowd favorite, as well. Learning to trim these shavings with a two-handed great axe can be rough going at first, but it's a rewarding process you'll learn to appreciate.

# Sleep Immunity

**Complexity: 1**  **Yields 1 cocktail**

Among the many things that elves are known for, perhaps one of the lesser-known qualities is their inherent sleeplessness and inability to be put in magical slumber. With this caffeine concoction, you can also feel what it's like to be one of these fair folk, at least for a time.

*2 ounces vodka*
*1 (8-ounce) can energy drink (larger is fine)*

1. Fill a highball glass with ice. Add vodka.
2. Slowly pour in energy drink.

> **DÜNGEONMEISTER TIP**
>
> Since its creation, this cocktail has been popular with those that wish to feel some of the power of Elvenkind flowing through them. There is a much less popular dwarven drink that lets you detect the slope of a floor—probably because it accomplishes this by being powerful enough to lay you flat out on the ground.

# Tiefling's Breakfast

**Complexity: 2**                                                     **Yields 1 cocktail**

Tieflings tend to eat like they live, with more than a little smoke, fire, and danger. This beverage serves as a morning pick-me-up that the fiendish among you can enjoy for its fiery heat and refreshing tang.

- 3/8 teaspoon celery salt, divided
- 2 lime wedges, divided
- 1½ ounces bourbon
- 1 teaspoon wasabi
- ¼ teaspoon hot sauce
- ¼ teaspoon Worcestershire sauce
- 2 ounces tomato juice
- 1 celery stalk, leaves on

1. Spread ⅛ teaspoon celery salt in a shallow dish. Use 1 lime wedge to moisten the rim of a pint glass, then dip the moistened rim into celery salt to coat lightly.

2. Fill glass with ice. Add remaining celery salt and all other ingredients except tomato juice, celery stalk, and remaining lime wedge.

3. Top with tomato juice and stir with a bar spoon. Garnish with celery stalk and lime wedge.

> **DÜNGEONMEISTER TIP**
>
> This is not the only drink to be named for the Tiefling race. In fact, there is one for every meal of the day. The Tiefling's Brunch tends to just be a mixture of champagne and catty gossip.

# Slippery Grippli

**Complexity: 2**　　　　　　　　　　　　　　　　　**Yields 1 shot**

If you're looking for green and slippery, you can't go wrong with the tiny batrachian swamp dwellers known as the Grippli. Masters of camouflage and ambush, these tiny creatures attack from the shadows in deadly flashes of emerald. To create this cocktail in their honor, a layered shooter provides swamp water (the brown schnapps), bulrushes (the tan Irish cream), and Frogfellow (green melon liqueur), all in one candy-sweet shot.

- ½ ounce butterscotch schnapps
- ¼ ounce Irish cream liqueur
- ½ ounce melon liqueur

1. Pour schnapps into a shot glass.
2. Slowly pour Irish cream over the back of a bar spoon into the glass to form a layer of cream over top of schnapps.
3. Repeat step 2 using melon liqueur over cream.

> **DÜNGEONMEISTER TIP**
>
> Applying any garnishes here would really be gilding the foxtail. Honestly, that's probably for the best, as the original garnish suggestions in the guidebook were two isopods on a toothpick and a hellgrammite at the bottom.

# Pixie Dust

**Complexity: 1**　　　　　　　　　　　　　　　　**Yields 1 cocktail**

Mischievous and mirthful, the pixie dust cocktail adds a touch of magic to any encounter, game or otherwise. A beautiful swirl of luster dust celebrates the arcane energies, and the delightful citrus combinations of soda, lemon, and elderflower bring a sharp acid sweetness to the palate. This drink may not have you sprouting wings, but it'll certainly leave you feeling like you're an inch or two off the ground.

- 1½ ounces vodka
- ½ ounce elderflower liqueur
- ¾ ounce lemon juice
- 2 ounces lemon-lime soda
- 1/16 teaspoon luster dust
- 1 stemmed maraschino cherry

1. Fill a champagne flute with cracked ice.
2. Add vodka, liqueur, lemon juice, and soda and stir with a swizzle stick. Add luster dust and briefly stir.
3. Spear cherry on a toothpick and add as garnish.

> **DÜNGEONMEISTER TIP**
>
> Remember, pixies are small in stature but still pack the same punch as any medium creature might, so imbibe these beverages with caution and respect. Disregarding the raw might of pixie dust is a great way to be excluded from next week's mushroom circle.

# Chapter 2

# CLASS-Y DRINKS

Looking to drink a cut above the rabble? Try mixing up a round of these character classics and share them around the table. Most folks are stuck with common drinks, but this chapter serves up a backstory, specialized training, and maybe even a familiar! With these libations, you're all set to start gaining levels. Or even to multiclass (multiclass only in moderation).

# Barbarian Rage

**Complexity: 1**  **Yields 1 cocktail**

Regardless of their homeland or upbringing, one thing all barbarian warriors have in common is the ability to call upon an all-consuming rage while in combat. With this combination of spirits and energy drink, you, too, can feel what it's like to be all brawn and no brains.

- 1 ounce vodka
- 1 ounce gin
- 1 ounce spiced rum
- 1 ounce light rum
- 1 ounce coconut rum
- 1 ounce tequila
- 1 ounce amaretto
- 1 ounce blue curaçao
- 1 ounce black raspberry liqueur
- 1 ounce melon liqueur
- 1 (8-ounce) can energy drink (larger is fine)

1. Fill a cocktail shaker with cracked ice. Add all ingredients except energy drink.
2. Shake and strain into a pint glass. Top with desired amount of energy drink.

> **DÜNGEONMEISTER TIP**
>
> In a pinch, the pint glass can be replaced with the skull of a recently defeated enemy. Be aware that this drink will cause you to fly into an energy-fueled mania of bad decisions where you may not be able to tell friend from foe. Before going into another rage, take a short rest.

# Bard's Songs

**Complexity: 1**  **Yields 6 cocktails**

When adventuring in the wilds or relaxing in a tavern, nothing can soothe the frayed nerves of a wanderer quite like a song from a bard. This drink has all the sparkle and glamour of the best showmen out there and is just as refreshing as kicking your feet up and listening to a great tune.

*8 ounces Pimm's No. 1 Cup*
*4 ounces gin*
*2 tablespoons lemon juice*
*2 tablespoons grenadine*
*32 ounces sparkling wine*
*1 cup fresh raspberries*

1. Place six champagne flutes in the freezer, allowing them to chill as you prepare the drink.

2. Fill a pitcher with ice. Add Pimm's No. 1 Cup, gin, lemon juice, and grenadine. Stir with a bar spoon until very cold, then strain equally into chilled flutes.

3. Fill each glass with equal amounts sparkling wine and raspberries.

> **DÜNGEONMEISTER TIP**
>
> One of the great arguments among the magic users of the world is whether a bard's song is actually magic or if they've somehow found a way to inspire through music in a way that seems magical. However, I once saw a bard get an ogre to dance a waltz with a halfling, so I'm going to say magic.

# Flavored Enemy

**Complexity: 1**  ⠀⠀⠀⠀⠀⠀⠀⠀⠀⠀⠀⠀⠀⠀⠀⠀⠀⠀⠀⠀⠀⠀⠀⠀⠀⠀**Yields 1 cocktail**

The rangers that wander the wilderness are known to have specific enemies that they study relentlessly, eventually getting to know their enemy in great detail. These enemies come in many different flavors, and this is just one flavor that you can master.

*1½ ounces vanilla vodka*
*3 ounces orange juice*
*½ teaspoon cranberry juice*
*1 orange wheel*

1. Fill a highball glass with ice. Add vodka and juices.
2. Stir with a bar spoon. Garnish with orange wheel.

> **DÜNGEONMEISTER TIP**
>
> The tradition among rangers to focus on a single type of enemy has a long and storied history. You see, one day, a ranger got lazy and decided to say that he only fought goblinoids so the local town would leave him alone about the nearby giants.

# Holy Water

**Complexity: 1**  **Yields 1 cocktail**

Holy water, when flung on a vampire or other intelligent undead, will repulse the creature and burn its vile hide as it shrinks away from the wielder. That said, actual holy water tastes like water, so it makes a lot of sense to hurl it at itinerant Draculas. This floral twist on the classic margarita tastes holy, so you may wish to retain it for consumption instead.

- 2 ounces reposado tequila
- 1 ounce elderflower liqueur
- 1 ounce lime juice
- 1 lime wheel

1. Place a cocktail glass in the freezer, allowing it to chill as you prepare the drink.
2. Fill a cocktail shaker with ice. Add all ingredients except lime wheel.
3. Shake and strain into chilled cocktail glass. Garnish with lime wheel.

> **DÜNGEONMEISTER TIP**
>
> Warning: Hurling this drink at a vampire will render his waistcoat and silly red cloak all sticky in the few seconds before he murders you, so consider offering him a glass instead.

# Necromancer

**Complexity: 1**             **Yields 1 cocktail**

The art of necromancy has often been looked down on as evil and unnatural. While this drink may seem to be as cloudy as the eyes of a newly risen corpse, it has a perfectly balanced flavor with citrusy strength.

- 1 ounce gin
- 1 ounce Cointreau
- 1 ounce Lillet Blanc
- 1 ounce lemon juice
- ⅛ teaspoon absinthe
- 1 orange twist (peel)

1. Place a coupe glass in the freezer, allowing it to chill as you prepare the drink.
2. Fill a cocktail shaker with ice. Add all ingredients except orange twist.
3. Shake and strain into chilled coupe glass. Garnish with orange twist.

> **DÜNGEONMEISTER TIP**
>
> Necromancers get a bad rap, and I can understand where most people are coming from. But, for us, there's honestly no one else we would rather turn to when we need somebody.

# Sneak Attack

**Complexity: 2**　　　　　　　　　　　　　　　　　　　**Yields 1 cocktail**

Rogues are known for being able to sneak up on the unsuspecting and take them out with one go. This is also true for this deceptively strong drink that masks its power in sweet and refreshing flavors.

2 ounces light rum
1¼ ounces maraschino liqueur
¾ ounce Cointreau
¾ ounce lime juice
¼ ounce simple syrup (see recipe in Tavern Basics)
½ cup crushed ice

1. Place a coupe glass in the freezer, allowing it to chill as you prepare the drink.
2. Place all ingredients in a blender. Blend on the pulse setting until smooth.
3. Pour into chilled coupe glass.

> **DÜNGEONMEISTER TIP**
>
> This drink used to be known as The Backstabber and was much more difficult to make. Over the years, more enlightened bartenders have made variations of it so that it is more accessible, if maybe less crushingly powerful. Some people still mistakenly call it the wrong name.

# Stunning Smite

**Complexity: 2**                                                       **Yields 1 cocktail**

Paladins can call upon their deity to help them smite evil and leave their foes stunned and reeling. This drink will smite what ails you as the warmth and sweetness spread, leaving all those you serve stunned by how good it is.

*For the Cinnamon Cider:*
½ cup apple cider
4 cinnamon sticks, divided

*For the Cocktail:*
1 ounce whiskey
½ ounce lemon juice
½ teaspoon maple syrup
3 apple slices

1. For the Cinnamon Cider: Combine cider and 3 cinnamon sticks in a small saucepan and cook over medium heat until simmering, approximately 3 minutes.
2. Turn off the heat and let mixture cool to room temperature.
3. For the Cocktail: Fill a cocktail shaker with ice. Add Cinnamon Cider, whiskey, lemon juice, and syrup to the shaker.
4. Fill a rocks glass with ice. Shake and strain whiskey mixture into the glass.
5. Garnish with apple slices and remaining cinnamon stick.

# Sweet and Sour-cerer

**Complexity: 1**　　　　　　　　　　　　　　　　**Yields 1 cocktail**

The sorcerer is a being of contrasts. They are bestowed with great power and yet have not learned how to properly use it. They are both mortal and yet something else. In the same way, this cocktail blends both sour and sweet into a drink that is more than it seems.

⅓ cup light rum
⅓ cup cherry liqueur
1 cup sweet and sour mix (see recipe in Tavern Basics)
1 lime wheel

1. Fill a cocktail shaker with ice. Add all ingredients except lime wheel.
2. Shake and strain into a highball glass filled with ice. Garnish with lime wheel.

> **DÜNGEONMEISTER TIP**
>
> "Sorcerers will try to tell you that they don't actually have any dragons in their ancestry and that it's actually just their inherent power. They are liars. Everyone knows that you only get magic powers without studying if your parents slept around with giant lizards." —A wizard

CHAPTER 2: CLASS-Y DRINKS | 53

# Gnomish Illusionist

**Complexity: 2**  **Yields 20 shots**

Gnomes of all stripes delight in matters and creatures of the deep earth. When gnomes lack ready access to either moles or molehills, a decadent party-pleaser treat like these Illusionists may suffice in a pinch. The confection combines alcohol with pudding to make a thick, rich treat that resembles the earth that gnomes possess an inherent connection to, and each is topped with a rainbow-striped illusion of a burrowing animal (like a gummy worm) to really make them feel homey.

*1 (3½-ounce) package instant chocolate pudding mix*
*¾ cup low-fat milk*
*¼ cup vodka*
*½ cup Irish cream liqueur*
*1 (8-ounce) container Cool Whip*
*1 (1½-ounce) bar milk or dark chocolate, shaved or crumbled*
*10 gummy worms, cut in half crosswise*

1. In a large mixing bowl, combine pudding mix and milk. Using a mixer on medium speed, mix until no lumps remain.
2. Stir in vodka and Irish cream.
3. Using a spatula, gently fold in Cool Whip.
4. Divide into individual shot glasses and top with pinches of shaved or crumbled chocolate bar and half of one gummy worm, pushed into the pudding.
5. Store in freezer until ready to serve.

# Sword and Chambord

**Complexity: 1**  **Yields 1 cocktail**

In the wilds of the land, there is little that a warrior can count on aside from their own strength and the weapons they wield. You must make sure everything is perfectly maintained, balanced, and sharp so that nothing fails you at the worst moment. This drink manages to strike that perfect balance of spicy, sweet, and strong that will leave you refreshed and ready for anything.

*2 ounces vodka*
*½ ounce black raspberry liqueur*
*½ ounce lime juice*
*4 ounces ginger beer*
*1 lime wheel*
*5 fresh raspberries*

1. Fill a Moscow mule mug with ice. Add vodka, liqueur, and lime juice.
2. Top with ginger beer. Garnish with lime wheel and raspberries scattered across the drink's surface.

### DÜNGEONMEISTER TIP

Those discerning drinkers who favor the taste of the Sword and Chambord cocktail will often have similar ideas on how it should be presented. Specifically, it is determined to be best when served in a tankard.

# Chapter 3

## SKILLED SELECTIONS

Dazzle your friends with a range of skillful cocktails. You can also use your mastery over these arts to embarrass your foes, since noncombat is the best way to avoid a fight. There's nothing secondary about our skills, so you can rest assured they're guaranteed to work. If you make your roll, anyway.

# Healing Surge

**Complexity: 1**  **Yields 1 cocktail**

Here's a blast of refreshing energy, a cool breeze that soothes the burn, and the pick-me-up you were looking for. This sour-sweet elixir will cure what ails you (please note that depending on the spell level of the user, this might only cure specifically any thirst that ails you).

- 1½ ounces tequila
- 1½ ounces sour apple liqueur
- 1 ounce lime juice
- ½ ounce simple syrup (see recipe in Tavern Basics)
- 5 ounces lemon-lime soda
- 1 slice Granny Smith apple

1. Fill a cocktail shaker with ice. Add all ingredients except soda and apple slice.
2. Shake and strain into a highball glass filled with ice, then top with soda. Garnish with apple slice.

### DÜNGEONMEISTER TIP

The best thing about this beverage is that consuming it is only a minor action, leaving you free to attack and move this round. Please only attack in moderation.

# Escape Artist

**Complexity: 1**  **Yields 1 cocktail**

Rogues are often possessed of a slippery talent to loosen their bonds and break their chains, sneaking free to pick pockets and find and remove traps again. To commemorate and encapsulate their greasy greatness, try the Escape Artist, a fresh, bright, herbaceous martini well lubricated with olive oil and vodka to keep things loose and law-scoffing.

*1 lemon wedge with peel*
*4 fresh basil leaves*
*4 ounces vodka*
*½ ounce simple syrup (see recipe in Tavern Basics)*
*½ ounce plus drizzle extra-virgin olive oil, divided*
*½ ounce dry vermouth*
*1 lemon twist (peel)*

1. Place a martini glass in the freezer, allowing it to chill as you prepare the drink.

2. Place lemon wedge and basil leaves in a mixing glass and muddle.

3. Add several ice cubes, vodka, syrup, ½ ounce olive oil, and vermouth to glass. Stir gently with a bar spoon.

4. Strain into chilled martini glass.

5. Drizzle remaining olive oil on top to form a small pool. Garnish with lemon twist.

# Point Blank Shot

**Complexity: 1**  **Yields 1 shot**

It takes a strong will as an archer to be able to remain cool and collected when someone comes running up to you with their sword out. Taking this shot will also require a steady hand and an open mind, as these two liquors combine into an entirely new flavor.

1½ ounces gin
¾ ounce whiskey
1 lemon twist (peel)

1. Fill a cocktail shaker with ice. Add gin and whiskey.
2. Shake and strain into a shot glass. Squeeze lemon twist over shot and hang twist on the rim as garnish.

> **DÜNGEONMEISTER TIP**
>
> There was a variation of this drink that was far less popular known as the Far Shot. It involved trying to throw a shot into a friend's mouth, and after many painful accidents, it was abandoned.

# Seduction Roll

**Complexity: 2**  **Yields 8 cocktails**

The art of seduction is a curious thing. There is no single thing that can make one seductive; it is a blend of many different factors. With all the different parts mixed together here, you get one singularly enticing drink that is sweet and tangy and leaves you wanting more.

*8 ounces vodka*
*16 ounces cranberry juice*
*3 tablespoons orange juice*
*4 ounces amaretto*
*2 tangerines, peeled and cut into 16 sections*

1. In a pitcher, combine vodka, juices, and amaretto and stir with a bar spoon.
2. Cover and chill until ready to serve.
3. Fill a cocktail shaker with ice. Add 1 cup of juice mixture.
4. Shake and strain into two martini glasses. Garnish each glass with 2 tangerine sections.
5. Repeat steps 3 and 4 three more times.

> **DÜNGEONMEISTER TIP**
>
> A Seduction Roll is romantic enough to potentially work on anyone. The nice thing is, with eight different chances, you're even more likely to find someone who thinks you're as special as your mother always says.

# Power Attack

**Complexity: 1**  **Yields 1 cocktail**

When fighting an enemy with more meat than brains, you sometimes need to sacrifice a little finesse for more raw power. While this drink seems sweet, fruity, and a little tart, it's packing a heck of a punch.

> 1 ounce Southern Comfort (you can substitute any good bourbon here, but be wary of alcohol content)
> ½ ounce vanilla vodka
> ½ ounce sloe gin
> ½ ounce Cointreau
> ½ ounce amaretto
> ½ ounce lemon juice
> 4 ounces orange juice
> 1 orange wedge

1. Fill a cocktail shaker with ice. Add all ingredients except orange juice and wedge.

2. Shake and strain into a cocktail glass filled with ice.

3. Top with orange juice and garnish with orange wedge.

### DÜNGEONMEISTER TIP

You don't always have to swing as hard as you can. Sometimes it's not right to do so. Sometimes you've got to line up a shot and get in flanking position. Sometimes you've got to wait. Sometimes you've got to swing late. Sometimes you've got to say, "Hey, I'm gonna smack you, softly."

# Royal Diplomacy

**Complexity: 1**  **Yields 1 cocktail**

In the courts and noble houses of the world, sometimes diplomacy can use a little bit of social lubrication to get the proceedings started. This deceivingly sweet drink can sneak up on you just like the best courtesan.

- ½ ounce blended whiskey (such as Crown Royal)
- ½ ounce Southern Comfort
- ½ ounce amaretto
- ½ ounce orange juice
- ½ ounce pineapple juice
- ½ ounce cranberry juice
- ½ teaspoon grenadine
- 1 orange wheel

1. Fill a cocktail shaker with ice. Add all ingredients except orange wheel.
2. Shake and strain into a cocktail glass filled with ice. Garnish with orange wheel.

> **DÜNGEONMEISTER TIP**
>
> It's often asked what the difference is between standard diplomacy and royal diplomacy. If you're being calm and gracious to get everyone to agree, that's regular diplomacy. If you're being calm and gracious to not get beheaded, that's royal diplomacy.

# Stealth Checks

**Complexity: 2**  **Yields 10 gelatin shots**

These innocuous shots may look like little more than clear, firm gin and tonics, and in fact they are just that. However, should they fall victim to the directed attention of a UV spot-check, they'll light up as bright as a rogue who should never have split the party. The secret? Quinine in the tonic water reacts to ultraviolet light in spectacular fluorescence.

- 1 cup plus 2 tablespoons tonic water
- 1 (¼-ounce) envelope unflavored powdered gelatin
- 2 tablespoons granulated sugar
- 6 ounces gin
- 1 tablespoon lime juice
- 1 tablespoon rose water

1. In a small saucepan over medium heat, bring tonic water to a boil.
2. Place gelatin and sugar in a medium heatproof bowl, then add boiled tonic water. Stir until completely dissolved, then set aside until cooled to room temperature, at least 40 minutes.
3. Stir in gin, lime juice, and rose water.
4. Divide mixture equally into ten shot glasses.
5. Refrigerate until set firm, at least 2 hours.
6. Serve in a dark room, using any sort of black light to create the glow effect.

# Turn Undead

**Complexity: 1**                                **Yields 1 cocktail**

When the dead rise up and threaten the living, only the holy clerics can stem the tide and cast back the horde. With this drink, you will find that the bitter and sour flavors that you might expect are turned into something much more pleasing.

> 1 ounce vodka
> 1 ounce coffee liqueur
> 2 teaspoons lemon juice

1. Fill an old-fashioned glass with ice. Add all ingredients.
2. Stir with a bar spoon.

> **DÜNGEONMEISTER TIP**
>
> There has been some confusion over the ability of Turn Undead. Often an embarrassed cleric or paladin will have to calmly explain that it is not, in fact, a way to join the ranks of the unliving. If one wishes to turn undead, it's probably wise to seek out a necromancer instead.

# Sprite of Hand

**Complexity: 1**                                                                    **Yields 2 shots**

A tricky cocktail for roguish sorts, the Sprite of Hand can do it all! It can dazzle, distract, pick pockets, and conceal small objects from view. (Those last two haven't been extensively tested.) With the complexity of whiskey providing a stiff back to the sweet and sour interplay of peach and citrus, this impressive beverage is sure to leave a mark (or at least clean out a mark's vulnerable pockets).

1 ounce Jameson (or other Irish whiskey)
1 ounce peach schnapps
1 ounce sweet and sour mix (see recipe in Tavern Basics)
1 ounce lemon-lime soda
2 lime wheels

1. Fill a cocktail shaker with ice. Add whiskey, schnapps, and sweet and sour mix.
2. Shake and strain into two shot glasses, filling each about three-quarters of the way.
3. Top with lemon-lime soda. Garnish with lime wheels.

> **DÜNGEONMEISTER TIP**
>
> Originally, a lockpick was used as a swizzle stick here, but the drink's glass profile is too low, and we are all *painfully* aware of how easily those things break. Plus, a truly talented rogue could open a locked chest with a lime. Probably.

CHAPTER 3: SKILLED SELECTIONS | 71

# Twin Strikes

**Complexity: 1**  **Yields 2 shots**

When you want to ensure that your foes will not escape unscathed, it's best to make sure your shot counts by coming at them from multiple angles. Similarly, this simple and effective shot comes at you with a sweetness from the liqueur and then follows up with the tartness of the lime.

*1½ ounces vodka*
*¾ ounce triple sec*
*¾ ounce lime juice*

1. Fill a cocktail shaker with ice. Add all ingredients.
2. Shake and strain into two shot glasses.

> **DÜNGEONMEISTER TIP**
>
> Many rangers practice to become ambidextrous so that they can dual wield with much more efficiency. This becomes an even more practical skill when attempting to get multiple drinks from the bar... to share with the party, of course.

# Chapter 4

# MAGIC MIXERS

You can have a little bit of magic right in your own home with these drinks straight out of a very drunken wizard's spell book. We've supplied the lists for all the material components you'll need to get started. The somatic component is drinking them, and the verbal component is going "Wooo!" while you do so.

# Acid Arrow

**Complexity: 1**  **Yields 1 shot**

There's something magical about this fruity and sweet blend of ingredients. Once mixed together, the herbal top helps to counter the spell of overwhelming sugar in the juice.

½ ounce coconut rum
¾ ounce pineapple juice
¼ ounce Jägermeister

1. Fill a cocktail shaker with ice. Add rum and pineapple juice. Shake and strain into a shot glass.

2. Slowly pour Jägermeister over the back of a bar spoon into the glass to form a layer over top of drink.

> **DÜNGEONMEISTER TIP**
>
> This shot to the head is certain to do some acidic damage. Just make sure your aim is correct when you let this one loose, or you could be dealing with some splash damage.

# Coors Light Wounds

**Complexity: 2**  **Yields 2 cocktails**

Even after a long rest, sometimes ailments linger on. If in great need, petition the local cleric to repair your aches and complaints through divine magic. Or, barring access to divine casters, try this smoky, spiced delight.

*2 tablespoons Tajín (or other chili spice blend)*
*2 tablespoons fine grain sea salt (or kosher salt)*
*½ teaspoon honey*
*2 ounces tomato juice*
*1 tablespoon lime juice*
*12 ounces Coors Light (or other beer)*
*1½ teaspoons chipotle hot sauce*
*1 teaspoon Worcestershire sauce*
*⅛ teaspoon soy sauce*

1. In a shallow dish, mix Tajín with salt. In a small dish, spread honey.

2. Dip the rims of two rocks glasses into honey, then dip the moistened rims into salt mixture to coat lightly. Fill both glasses with ice.

3. In a pitcher, combine all remaining ingredients and stir with a bar spoon. Pour into prepared glasses.

> **DÜNGEONMEISTER TIP**
>
> This concoction is rumored to ease your passage from even the most harrowing hangover. If you don't have any Coors Light on hand, congratulations! Give yourself 250 XP for not being burdened with cheap American lager.

# Elemental Plane of Fire

**Complexity: 2**  **Yields 1 punch bowl (serves 6)**

On the Plane of Fire, there is no escape from the intense heat and the flames that threaten to consume everything. While not quite as inescapable as its namesake, this Elemental Plane of Fire will give you a spicy kick while still delivering a tangy, tasty treat.

- 2 tablespoons Tajín (or other chili spice blend)
- 2 tablespoons fine grain sea salt (or kosher salt)
- 1 small seedless watermelon (~5 pounds), cubed (roughly 8 cups cubed fruit)
- 7 lime wedges, divided
- 2 cups sparkling water
- 8 ounces lime juice
- 16 ounces tequila
- ⅓ cup granulated sugar
- 2 jalapeños, seeded and sliced

1. In a shallow dish, mix Tajín with salt. Rub 1 lime wedge around the rims of 6 punch glasses, then dip the moistened rims into salt mixture to coat lightly.

2. Place watermelon and sparkling water in a blender and blend until smooth, approximately 30–45 seconds.

3. Strain watermelon mixture through a sieve into a punch bowl.

4. Add lime juice, tequila, sugar, and jalapeño slices to bowl and stir with a bar spoon. Chill until ready to serve.

5. Pour beverage into prepared glasses with ice. Add remaining lime wedges to rims of glasses.

# Black Mana

**Complexity: 2**                          **Yields 1 cocktail**

Seeking something a little sinister? Try out a Black Mana, the coalesced essence of death, decay, and subversion. Sure, that might not sound like an appetizing start to a cocktail, but good news abounds, because the denizens of eternal night like coffee drinks as much as we do, if not more. This sweet midnight draft will keep you going through hours of grave-bound machinations.

*3 ounces vanilla vodka*
*1 ounce coffee liqueur*
*1 ounce crème de cacao*
*1 ounce chilled espresso*
*½ teaspoon powdered activated charcoal*

1. Place a martini glass in the freezer, allowing it to chill as you prepare the drink.

2. Fill a cocktail shaker with ice. Add vodka, liqueur, and crème de cacao. Shake and strain into chilled martini glass.

3. Top with espresso and activated charcoal and stir with a bar spoon.

# Green Mana

**Complexity: 1**  **Yields 1 cocktail**

The magical influences of wild places, the spiritual energy that lives in leaf, soil, and creature alike . . . green mana is nature made manifest. To appreciate the best it has to offer, try this enchanting blend of melon, mint, and lime, which will set your mind to all things natural and your soul to birdsong.

- 15 fresh mint leaves, divided
- ¾ ounce melon liqueur
- ¾ ounce lime juice
- 1½ ounces light rum
- 2 ounces club soda

1. Place 10 mint leaves and liqueur in a cocktail shaker and muddle.
2. Add lime juice and rum, then fill the shaker with ice. Shake and strain into a rocks glass filled with ice.
3. Top with club soda and stir with a bar spoon. Garnish with remaining mint leaves.

> **DÜNGEONMEISTER TIP**
>
> The original version of this cocktail also contained 2 tablespoons of assorted spider parts and most of an ape. We've modified the beverage into a vegetarian blend out of respect for nature (and because the apes kept eating the good spider parts).

# Faerie Fire

**Complexity: 2**                                                   **Yields 1 cocktail**

Sparks and glitter in the darkness of the swamp portend mischievous ghosts, protective nature spirits, or secretive druids conducting ancient rituals. In this orange-essence blue beverage, they merely portend the presence of sparkling LED ice cubes.

*2 ounces blue curaçao*
*1½ ounces gin*
*1 ounce sweet vermouth*
*½ ounce orange juice*
*1 or 2 LED flashing ice cubes*
*1 orange wheel*

1. Fill a cocktail shaker with ice. Add all ingredients except LED ice cubes and orange wheel.

2. Shake and pour into a hurricane glass with LED ice cubes inside. Garnish with orange wheel.

### DÜNGEONMEISTER TIP

There are a variety of ways to acquire glowing, blinking ice cubes. You can seek the services of friendly enchanters, trap the spirit of a lantern ghost on a midwinter's night, or—by far the most common—get them online, since they generally run a dozen for about $12.

# Hpnotiq Pattern

**Complexity: 1**                                                    **Yields 1 cocktail**

A clever mage knows that you don't have to kill your opponent when you can much more easily dazzle them with a swirling, colorful display. When these two liquids mix, you get a lustrous, swirling, color-changing concoction that has a fruity and unique flavor.

> 3 ounces crushed ice
> 1 ounce Hpnotiq or other lustrous swirling liqueur
> 1 ounce cognac

1. Fill a cocktail glass with ice.
2. Pour Hpnotiq first and then cognac over ice. Stir with a bar spoon.

> **DÜNGEONMEISTER TIP**
>
> The interesting thing about a spell that mesmerizes all who look at it is that nobody can really remember what the pattern in question actually looks like. There have been varying loose accounts with some saying it looked like a human infant that was dancing and others saying the pattern took the form of a clothed feline playing some manner of keyed instrument.

# Blue Mana

**Complexity: 1**                                    **Yields 1 cocktail**

The fury of the seas, the rush of the breeze, and the quiet contemplation of the scholar all embody the complexity of blue mana. So, too, can this combination of sweet, sour, and bitter be swirled together into a concoction that is bound to be an inspiration.

*2 tablespoons granulated sugar*
*1 lime wedge*
*2 ounces cranberry juice*
*½ ounce lime juice*
*1 ounce vodka*
*1 ounce blue curaçao*
*½ teaspoon pearl luster dust*

1. Spread sugar in a shallow dish. Rub lime wedge around the rim of a rocks glass, then dip the moistened rim into sugar to coat lightly.

2. Fill a cocktail shaker with ice. Add juices, vodka, and curaçao.

3. Shake and strain into prepared glass. Sprinkle luster dust over cocktail.

### DÜNGEONMEISTER TIP

Mages who favor the use of blue mana are famous (or perhaps infamous) for their reliance upon countermagic. It is said that you can always tell when two great blue wizards are dueling by the lack of anything happening.

# Red Mana

**Complexity: 1**  **Yields 1 cocktail**

When you consider a cocktail based on destructive fury, flame, and stone, and aggressive creatures of mountain and warren, whiskey immediately comes to mind. A fiery blend that soothes as it burns, the Red Mana is a challenging drink that you should tap into. For one damage.

- 2 ounces cinnamon whiskey
- 2 ounces apple whiskey
- 1 teaspoon grenadine
- 2 ounces club soda
- 1 small Thai chili

1. Fill a cocktail shaker with ice. Add whiskeys and grenadine.
2. Shake and strain into a cocktail glass filled with ice.
3. Top with club soda and stir. Garnish with chili.

> **DÜNGEONMEISTER TIP**
>
> Many times a goblin raiding party has made its way into the lands of man and caused swaths of destruction. Nobody is sure what spurs the goblins to do this, but the most credible idea postulated so far is that it's the result of drunken dares taken entirely too far.

# White Mana

**Complexity: 1**  **Yields 2 cocktails**

White mana is the essence of purity, civilization, and teamwork (which is of course why this recipe makes two servings). Naturally, these things, when distilled and combined into a beverage, will taste like upscale party-friendly chocolate milk. Offer this sweet celebratory drink to the angel in your life.

- 2 tablespoons granulated sugar
- 2 tablespoons water
- 8 ounces chocolate vodka
- ½ cup sweetened condensed milk

1. Spread sugar in a shallow dish. Add water to a small bowl. Dip the rims of two martini glasses into water, then dip the moistened rims into sugar to coat lightly.

2. Fill a cocktail shaker with ice. Add vodka and condensed milk. Shake and strain into prepared glasses.

> **DÜNGEONMEISTER TIP**
>
> For additional white mana perfection, allow us to offer a serving suggestion. This drink pairs well with at least fifteen little cocktail weenies.

CHAPTER 4: MAGIC MIXERS | 89

# Magic Mistletoe

**Complexity: 2**  **Yields 1 cocktail**

Even in a world of magic and monsters, it's still nice to be able to celebrate a holiday with those you love and appreciate the flavors and smells of winter. With a little mixology magic, you can create a drink that will give the gift of smiles and look good doing it.

- 15 fresh cranberries, divided
- 2 orange half-wheels
- 2 ounces London Dry gin
- 1 ounce simple syrup (see recipe in Tavern Basics)
- 1 LED flashing ice cube
- 3 ounces cranberry juice
- 1½ ounces club soda
- 1 thyme sprig

1. Place 7 cranberries and orange half-wheels in a Collins glass and muddle.
2. Add gin and syrup and fill the glass with ice, including LED cube.
3. Top with cranberry juice and club soda. Stir with thyme sprig and garnish with remaining cranberries.

> **DÜNGEONMEISTER TIP**
>
> Nobody can quite remember why it is that mistletoe became a traditional decoration in the winter months. Wizards have said that it may have been a component of an ancient ritual spell that would help attack the darkness in the long winter nights.

# Psionic Blasts

**Complexity: 2**  **Yields 6 shots**

A ripping blast of raw mental energy, the psionic blast is the mind mage's most overwhelming and powerful attack. These shots maintain the crackling halo of a psionic at full force, while thoughtfully reducing the mental damage by several orders of magnitude.

> 2 tablespoons vanilla frosting
> 1 (⅓-ounce) package popping candy
> 3 ounces vodka
> 3 ounces blue curaçao
> 3 ounces lime juice

1. Spread frosting in a shallow dish. In another small dish, spread candy. Dip the rims of six shot glasses into frosting, then dip the frosted rims into candy to coat lightly.

2. Fill a cocktail shaker with ice. Add vodka, curaçao, and lime juice. Shake and strain into prepared shot glasses.

> **DÜNGEONMEISTER TIP**
>
> If you find your intellect fortress assailed by these libations, consider switching to water for the duration of the evening. Your memories will remain, and you will thank yourself in the morning.

CHAPTER 4: MAGIC MIXERS | 93

# Peanut Butter & Jellikinesis

**Complexity: 2**　　　　　　　　　　　　　　　　**Yields 1 cocktail**

One of the fringe benefits to sorcery is the innate capacity to prepare concoctions without dirtying a dish. By levitating the ingredients and applying them to bread, even a starting sorcerer can assemble a sandwich without cleaning a bread knife. This cocktail, which calls to mind the classic flavor of the world's most famous sandwich (citation needed), can at least come close.

- 2 ounces peanut butter whiskey
- ½ ounce grape jelly simple syrup (see recipe in Tavern Basics)
- ⅛ teaspoon salt
- 2 slices sourdough bread (or bread of your choice)
- 2 tablespoons peanut butter
- 2 tablespoons Concord grape jelly

1. Place a large ice cube or ice ball in a rocks glass.
2. Combine whiskey, syrup, and salt in the glass. Stir with a bar spoon.
3. Use remaining ingredients to make a peanut butter and jelly sandwich. Cut finished sandwich into roughly ½" squares. Spear one square on a toothpick and add as garnish.

> **DÜNGEONMEISTER TIP**
>
> Match your drink to your sorcerous subclass. Draconic heritage the source of your magical potential? Bring some flame breath to the party with jalapeño-peach jelly in the simple syrup.

# Goodberries

**Complexity: 2**  **Yields 4 cocktails**

When needed, Druids can magically conjure an entire meal's worth of nutrition within a single berry. Now, you, too, can create an enchantingly strong beverage. With all the flavor of sweet berries and a little tartness for balance.

¼ cup superfine sugar
2 tablespoons water
½ cup goodberry syrup (see recipe in Tavern Basics)
4 ounces lime juice
8 ounces blanco tequila
Assorted fresh berries
4 lime wheels

1. Spread sugar in a shallow dish. Add water to a small bowl.

2. Dip the rims of four cocktail glasses into water, then dip the moistened rims into sugar to coat lightly.

3. Fill a cocktail shaker with ice. Add syrup, lime juice, and tequila.

4. Shake and strain into prepared glasses filled with ice.

5. Skewer four sets of berries. Garnish each glass with skewered berries and a lime wheel.

> **DÜNGEONMEISTER TIP**
>
> Philosophers have long wondered what it means to be good. If a berry can be said to be good, then should we not also be? Does the existence of a goodberry necessitate the hidden threat of the evilberry?

# Chapter 5

# MUDDLED MINIONS

These threats may be diminutive, but they certainly aren't minor. Inspired by the dungeon denizens that are down there in the dark putting in the hard days to make delves scary for adventurers, each of these cocktails packs a punch that's well above its weight class—or its challenge rating, for that matter.

# Gelatinous Cubes

**Complexity: 3**　　　　　　　　　　　　　　**Yields 10 gelatin shots**

The translucent dungeon abomination known as the gelatinous cube is famous for deceiving adventurers into ignoring it until it's too late. Then, of course, it dissolves them into a thin nutrient paste. These adorable cinnamon shots can also sneak up on you, so "consume mindlessly" in moderation.

*2 cups chilled water*
*2 cups granulated sugar*
*4 (¼-ounce) envelopes unflavored powdered gelatin*
*16 ounces chilled Goldschläger*
*2 drops green food coloring*

1. In a small saucepan over medium heat, combine water and sugar and stir. Bring to a simmer and swirl pan until sugar is completely dissolved (do not stir the sugar water, just swirl the pan).

2. Remove from heat and add gelatin, whisking until gelatin is dissolved. Add the Goldschläger, pour into a medium baking dish, and stir. Add food coloring to create slime appearance.

3. Stir again to agitate gold flakes.

4. Chill for at least 2 hours or until fully set.

5. Slice into ten cubes.

# Giant Bee

**Complexity: 1**  **Yields 1 cocktail**

Sometimes the deadliest monsters make the most delightful drinks. The Giant Bee is a charmingly packaged delivery mechanism for the complexities of good gin and the subtle toothsome sweetness of honey, but beware; it packs a citrusy sting. It may be a random encounter the first time, but after a few sips, you'll want this beverage as a familiar.

> 2 ounces gin
> ¾ ounce honey syrup (*see recipe in Tavern Basics*)
> 1 ounce lemon juice
> 1 lemon wedge

1. Fill a cocktail shaker with ice. Add all ingredients.
2. Shake and strain into a rocks glass. Garnish with lemon wedge.

### DÜNGEONMEISTER TIP

If the Giant Bee proves insufficient as a challenge to your party, consider the following template to give it more body, power, bite, and hit points as needed.
- The Dire Bee: Substitute hot honey syrup for honey syrup.

# Goblin Grenades

**Complexity: 3**  **Yields 12 shots**

These evil little green monsters are anything but subtle. A zesty-sweet combination of jalapeño and strawberry, each shot has a spicy zing to it that you might find delightful until it blows up like the ramshackle concoction it is. For maximum chaos, this beverage is served directly in a jalapeño, rimmed with extra spice for extra pain. And just like the genuine goblinoid article, these little sneaks travel in numbers.

*For the Shot Glasses:*
12 jalapeños
2 tablespoons Tajín (or other chili spice blend)
½ lime, juiced

*For the Cocktail:*
1 lime, zested and juiced
2 cups hulled and sliced strawberries
¼ cup granulated sugar
¼ cup water
1 jalapeño, seeded and sliced
2 ounces lemon vodka

1. For the Shot Glasses: Cut the tops off jalapeños and use a spoon or knife to remove seeds and whites from inside.

2. Spread Tajín in a shallow dish. Add lime juice to a small bowl.

3. Dip each jalapeño into lime juice, then dip in Tajín to coat the rim of the jalapeño.

4. Set aside to dry.

5. For the Cocktail: In a medium saucepan over medium heat, combine lime juice and zest, strawberries, sugar, water, and jalapeño slices and cook for 5 minutes. Allow to cool slightly.

6. Transfer to a blender and pulse once.

7. Strain mixture through a fine-mesh sieve into a large cocktail shaker.

8. Add vodka to strained mixture and chill in the refrigerator until ready to serve.

9. Shake and strain into each prepared jalapeño.

> **DÜNGEONMEISTER TIP**
>
> Consider placing each jalapeño inside a convenient shot glass that you could have just used in the first place. A great way to serve them is to fill a bowl with little chocolate candies and stand each loaded jalapeño shooter upright among them. Just keep a sharp eye out, as any halfway competent goblin will steal your candies, your bowl, and probably blow up your dog on the way out.

# Illithid Substance

**Complexity: 2**  **Yields 1 cocktail**

Mind flayers are utterly and terrifyingly inhuman, and so are their bars. There's loose brain matter slopping out of highball glasses everywhere; the lighting is dim to the point of near darkness, only occasionally punctuated by mind-addling strobe flashes from nowhere; and the jukebox selection is all Counting Crows B-sides. Of course there are good reasons to visit, too, among them this apple and whiskey concoction, which is sour, sweet, and swirling with psychic residue.

> 2 ounces Irish whiskey
> 1½ ounces sour apple liqueur
> ½ ounce lemon juice
> ½ ounce simple syrup (see recipe in Tavern Basics)
> ¼ teaspoon gold luster dust

1. Fill a cocktail shaker with ice. Add all ingredients.
2. Shake and strain into a highball glass. Garnish with a swizzle stick.

### DÜNGEONMEISTER TIP

Like virtually every other object or substance dreamed up or concocted by a mind flayer, this beverage was not meant to last in our reality for long. The luster within it will rapidly settle to the bottom in a puddle of silty dust without regular agitation.

# 1d3 Wandering Minstrels

**Complexity: 1**  **Yields 1 shot**

If you've gone wandering through the countryside, then you know how inevitable it is that you will eventually run into one to three wandering minstrels when you least expect it. Similarly, this drink can blindside you when three different whiskeys all blend together in one place. Enjoy, as much as anyone can enjoy wandering minstrels.

½ ounce Scotch whisky
½ ounce Tennessee whiskey
½ ounce bourbon

1. Fill a cocktail shaker with ice. Add all ingredients.
2. Shake and strain into a shot glass.

### DÜNGEONMEISTER TIP

Of course I hear you say, "But it's 1d3 Wandering Minstrels! Why does it always have three?!" Far be it from us to tell you how to enjoy your whiskey. If you want, roll a d3 and then reduce the different alcohols accordingly.

# Kobold Fashioned

**Complexity: 1**  **Yields 1 cocktail**

The yapping, snapping, and trap-making of the common kobold can be infuriating to those who are forced to live near them, especially the dragons they tend to live in service of. Those dragons need a libation to take their mind off the latest round of some minor clan chieftain inventing the "skunk on a pole" or some similar act of tomfoolery. Such dragons can at least count on kobold bar chiefs, who may only know how to make one cocktail, but it's a trusted classic.

 1 sugar cube
 ¼ teaspoon aromatic bitters
 1½ tablespoons water
 1½ ounces rye whiskey
 1 lime twist (peel)
 1 stemmed maraschino cherry

1. Place sugar cube in an old-fashioned glass and sprinkle with bitters.
2. Add water and muddle until dissolved, adding more water if needed.
3. Fill the glass with ice cubes and add whiskey. Stir with a bar spoon.
4. Spear lime twist and cherry on a toothpick and add as garnish.

# Mermaid Lagoon

**Complexity: 1**  **Yields 1 punch bowl (serves 6)**

Mermaids (both good and bad) find homes in clear blue pools. Anyone who comes across this refreshing, tropical lagoon of flavor will definitely want to dive right in, and risks be damned.

- 4 ounces blue curaçao
- 2 ounces melon liqueur
- 1 (750-milliliter) bottle prosecco
- 12 ounces pineapple juice
- 8 ounces light rum
- 2 (12-ounce) cans seltzer
- 2½ cups pineapple chunks, divided
- 16 stemmed maraschino cherries, divided
- Edible flowers for garnish (optional)

1. Fill a punch bowl halfway with ice. Add curaçao and liqueur.
2. Top with prosecco, pineapple juice, rum, and seltzer. Mix.
3. Add in half the pineapple chunks and 10 halved cherries.
4. Skewer remaining pineapple and cherries on six skewers and add as garnish on punch cups. Add edible flowers to punch bowl if desired.

> **DÜNGEONMEISTER TIP**
>
> This drink is so alluring that it has been known to shipwreck sailors, crashing into rocks. We don't know who put it out on some jagged rocks in the first place. Did they want their drink . . . on the rocks?

# Troll Slobber

**Complexity: 1**  **Yields 1 cocktail**

Out in the swamps and forests of the untamed wilderness, you can tell when you come across a troll's home from the distinctive goo left behind. Don't worry, though: This sweet and bubbly version trades in the regenerative slime for a tangy, creamy lime flavor.

- 2 scoops lime sherbet
- 2 ounces pineapple rum
- 5 ounces lemon-lime soda
- 2 stemmed maraschino cherries

1. Scoop sherbet into a tall glass. Add rum and soda.
2. Stir gently with a bar spoon to create a cloudy bottom. Note: Over-stirring will pop the bubbles.
3. The top will foam. Once it does, garnish with cherries.

> **DÜNGEONMEISTER TIP**
>
> There is a rumor that the slobber of a troll can impart some of their astounding regenerative abilities to anyone brave enough to imbibe it. That rumor was started by Trandish the Bard when trying to trick his friend into drinking troll spit and was, by all accounts, hilarious.

# Wight Russian

**Complexity: 1**  **Yields 1 cocktail**

Whiskey supplants vodka in this death-defying variation on the classic White Russian, in no small part because whiskey is the core spirit choice of intelligent undead everywhere (this is a well-known fact—just ask any mummy). This creamy concoction will send a paralytic chill down your spine.

> 1 ounce chilled coffee
> 1 ounce coffee liqueur
> 1 ounce white whiskey
> ½ cup heavy cream
> ⅛ teaspoon orange bitters
> 1 orange twist (peel)

1. Place an old-fashioned glass in the freezer, allowing it to chill as you prepare the drink.

2. Fill a cocktail shaker with ice. Add coffee, liqueur, and whiskey. Shake and strain into chilled old-fashioned glass.

3. Top with cream and bitters. Twist orange peel over the glass to express orange oils.

# Gin and Skeletonic

**Complexity: 1**  **Yields 1 cocktail**

Finally, a drink a skeleton could enjoy! Well, maybe not; it's still just gonna pour right through them, right? But at least it's pretty, colorful, and even refreshing if you have a tongue and esophagus. The bitter orange notes from the Aperol serve well as a chilling reminder of the many things a skeleton can no longer enjoy in their undeath, while the grapefruit provides a chilling heart-healthy source of lycopene.

- 1½ ounces Aperol
- ½ ounce gin
- 1 teaspoon simple syrup (see recipe in Tavern Basics)
- 1½ ounces tonic water
- 1½ ounces grapefruit juice
- 5 whole white peppercorns

1. Fill a cocktail shaker with ice. Add Aperol, gin, and syrup.
2. Shake and strain into an ice-filled tall glass. Top with tonic water and grapefruit juice.
3. Garnish with white peppercorns.

### DÜNGEONMEISTER TIP

While the white peppercorns work well as a little reminder of bones in the beverage, this one is really all about presentation. A skull goblet will go a long way toward driving home the point here, and heck, you could even stir this with a big old bone if you want.

CHAPTER 5: MUDDLED MINIONS | 115

# Rust Monster

**Complexity: 1**  **Yields 1 cocktail**

The bane of fighters everywhere, the rust monster can quickly turn even the sturdiest armor and shields to so much oxidized dust and ruin. Canny adventurers are quick to avoid these chitinous terrors, but the drink that bears their name is hard to avoid. Complexities abound in this herbal, unusual variation on the traditional rusty nail.

- 2 ounces mezcal
- 1 ounce Drambuie

Place a large ice cube in a rocks glass. Add mezcal and Drambuie and stir.

> **DÜNGEONMEISTER TIP**
>
> It would be highly inadvisable to serve this particular cocktail in a mule mug, or any metal container for that matter, unless you're not thirsty and have a preponderance of paper towels around.

# Chapter 6

## IMMENSE INTOXICANTS

The most dangerous foes require the most delightful beverages, and that's what you'll find here. Whether you're looking for something fiery, fruity, or festive, you'll be sure to find it represented among these classically deadly enemies of dungeon antiquity. You'll want to bring a whole party to face these challenges!

# The 666 Layers of the Abyss, Now with Coconut

**Complexity: 2**  **Yields 1 cocktail**

The secret to this blended beverage lies in the dark juice of fresh cherries, which, when whirled together with coconut cream, can form beautiful striations on par with the layers of the underworld itself, each more fiendish than the one above. As an added bonus, they add a rich fruity note to the whole affair instead of the screams of an infinite army of twisted demonic wretches.

> 1 cup ice cubes
> 10 stemmed and pitted fresh dark cherries (such as Bing or Sweetheart)
> ½ ounce cherry syrup
> ¼ cup coconut cream
> 2 ounces pineapple juice
> 2 ounces light rum
> 1 tablespoon whipped cream
> 1 pineapple wedge

1. Place all ingredients except whipped cream and pineapple wedge in a blender and blend on the pulse setting until combined, approximately 15–20 seconds.

2. Pour into a highball glass. Garnish with whipped cream and pineapple wedge.

### DÜNGEONMEISTER TIP

This drink should never be served alongside a Nine Hells cocktail, unless you want blood all over your nice tablecloth—in which case go right ahead.

# Breath Weapon

**Complexity: 1**                                **Yields 1 cocktail**

The cunning and devious green dragons make their lairs deep in the woods, ready to spew a cloud of poison gas at any adventurers who might challenge them. While not as powerful as an ancient wyrm, this twist on the classic martini will make people take notice in a 60-foot cone.

*2 ounces vodka*
*½ ounce dry vermouth*
*½ teaspoon juice from jar of garlic-stuffed olives*
*1 garlic-stuffed olive*
*1 clove pickled garlic*

1. Place a martini glass in the freezer, allowing it to chill as you prepare the drink.

2. Fill a cocktail shaker with ice. Add vodka, vermouth, and olive juice.

3. Shake and strain into chilled martini glass. Spear olive and garlic on a toothpick and add as garnish.

> **DÜNGEONMEISTER TIP**
>
> In addition to the standard breath attack of a dragon, this drink can also imbue you with the frightful presence that wyrms are known for. Just imbibe the drink in front of someone and then start to move uncomfortably close. It's guaranteed to cause terror.

# Nature Goddess

**Complexity: 2**  **Yields 8 cocktails**

Possessed of a bountiful harvest? This cool and refreshing drink will combine the best of summer while cooling you down. Praise your nature god of choice, or at least pour a little out to keep the festering gods of decay at bay . . . for now.

*¼ cup fresh mint leaves*
*1 rosemary sprig*
*4 ounces vodka*
*2 cups lemon-lime soda*
*3 oranges, sliced into wheels*
*1½ cups cucumber wheels*

1. Place mint and rosemary in a pitcher and muddle.
2. Pour in vodka and soda and stir with a bar spoon.
3. Place 3 alternating orange and cucumber wheels at the bottom of eight large glasses, then add ice.
4. Pour beverage into glasses and serve.

### DÜNGEONMEISTER TIP

If your nature goddess is one of those "full cycle of death and rebirth" types of goddesses, this drink can be easily adapted to properly praise and raise glory unto them as well. Just alternate wheel-chopped shiitake mushrooms in among the cucumber and orange.

# Claw Claw Snakebite

**Complexity: 1**                                    **Yields 1 cocktail**

Besides their raw strength, one of the things that makes monsters like manticores and chimeras so powerful is that they have multiple means of attack. Just like a chimera, the layered attacks from this drink will definitely pack a one-two punch that is sure to be a knockout.

> 12 ounces dry cider
> 12 ounces dark beer

1. Pour cider slowly into a pint glass.
2. Slowly pour dark beer over the back of a bar spoon into the glass to form a layer over top of cider.

> **DÜNGEONMEISTER TIP**
>
> With the sharp claws of a lion and the fiery breath of a dragon, it's no wonder people often ignore the goat part of the chimera. But that's fine. The goat part was ignoring you too. It doesn't feel bad. It likes being forgotten. Shut up. No, you're crying.

# Dragon the Beach

**Complexity: 1**                                                    **Yields 1 cocktail**

Dragons obviously like hitting the shore. Sure, they're mostly there to devour dolphins and unsuspecting anglers, but everyone has a different way of finding a good time. In this case, a classic beverage is brought to fiery life with a dash of spice, combining the cool of the water with the heat of the sun . . . and the breath weapons.

- 2 ounces vodka
- 1 ounce peach schnapps
- 2 ounces grapefruit juice
- 2 ounces cranberry juice
- ½ teaspoon hot honey syrup (*see recipe in Tavern Basics*)

Fill a highball glass with ice. Add all ingredients and stir with bar spoon.

> **DÜNGEONMEISTER TIP**
>
> If you're concerned about the heat, you can always omit the hot honey syrup in favor of regular honey syrup. At that point, however, this drink is just the classic sex on the beach, and we can't imagine whom that would even conceptually appeal to.

# Mai Tyrant

**Complexity: 2**  **Yields 1 cocktail**

Distilling the essence of a Beholder's eye rays isn't easy. First of all, there's, like, ten of them and they all do something different. Second, most of what they do isn't especially pleasant, drink or otherwise. No one wants a paralytic beverage or a disintegration shot, after all.

- ½ cup cubed seedless watermelon
- 3 tablespoons light rum
- 2 tablespoons elderflower liqueur
- 1 tablespoon lime juice
- 1 tablespoon superfine sugar
- 2 seedless grapes

1. Place all ingredients except grapes in a blender and blend on high for 30 seconds.
2. Pour into a rocks glass. Spear grapes on the end of two bendable drinking straws and add as garnish.

> **DÜNGEONMEISTER TIP**
>
> Make sure to save and reuse those drinking straws! Being bent on total mental domination of all sentient life doesn't mean you shouldn't do your part for the planet. It's the only one we've got, you know.

# Purple Worm

**Complexity: 2**          **Yields 1 cocktail**

This beast of a beverage is as sharp-toothed and fearsome as the mindless monster that bears its name. A deep indigo body full of berry and citrus flavors is far preferable to the half-melted slag and unfortunate miner carcasses that fill the belly of the real thing, however. Much like the colossal cnidarian, we've rimmed the mouth of the cocktail with green, but luckily, it's just decorating sugar, not festering acid.

- 2 tablespoons green decorating sugar
- 2 tablespoons plus 1 ounce cranberry juice (or cran-grape or grape juice), divided
- 1½ ounces vodka
- 1 ounce blue curaçao
- 1 ounce sweet and sour mix (see recipe in Tavern Basics)
- 1 ounce grenadine
- 1 teaspoon silver luster dust

1. Spread sugar in a shallow dish. Add 2 tablespoons cranberry juice to a small bowl.

2. Dip the rim of a highball glass into cranberry juice, then dip the moistened rim into sugar to coat lightly.

3. Fill a cocktail shaker with ice. Add vodka, curaçao, sweet and sour mix, grenadine, remaining cranberry juice, and luster dust.

4. Shake and strain into prepared glass with ice.

# Silver Dragon

**Complexity: 2**　　　　　　　　　　　　　　　　**Yields 1 cocktail**

The silver dragon is unique among its fellows in that it is one of the few dragons that enjoys the company of human and elf, so much so that it will often transform to look like them and spend time among them. This effervescent and bubbly drink is also best in the company of friends, but, like its namesake, remains regal and often hard to find.

- 2 ounces dry gin
- 1 ounce lemon juice
- 1 teaspoon superfine sugar
- 1 large pasteurized egg white
- 1 (12-ounce) can club soda

1. Place a Collins glass in the freezer, allowing it to chill as you prepare the drink.
2. Fill cocktail shaker with ice. Add all ingredients except club soda.
3. Shake and strain into chilled Collins glass and top with club soda. Serve with a stirring rod.

> **DÜNGEONMEISTER TIP**
>
> Oftentimes, a silver dragon will take on the shape of a human to participate in their favorite things, such as feasts. If you suspect there may be a dragon at your local holiday feast, try to spot the person putting all the silverware in a pile in front of them.

# Release the Kraken

**Complexity: 2**  **Yields 1 cocktail**

From the depths of the ocean comes a frightful beast that all sailors know and fear. When unleashed, there is no escaping from its grasp. Similarly, once you get a hold of this drink, you'll never want to let it out of your grasp. When the sweet and citrus flavors combine with the sour "tentacles," you'll see why the kraken is so infamous.

- 2 ounces dark rum
- 1½ ounces blue curaçao
- 6 ounces pineapple juice
- 2 ounces orange juice
- 1 cup ice cubes
- 4 sour gummy worms

1. Place a highball glass in the freezer, allowing it to chill as you prepare the drink.
2. Place all ingredients except gummy worms in a blender and pulse until slushy and combined, approximately 15–20 seconds.
3. Pour into chilled highball glass. Arrange gummy worms throughout to represent tentacles.

> **DÜNGEONMEISTER TIP**
>
> The kraken itself has been depicted in many different forms—sometimes as a giant squid or other tentacled beast, and sometimes as a giant claymation creature from the black lagoon with four arms. Such is the mystery and majesty of the mighty beast.

# Girallon and On

**Complexity: 1**                                                       **Yields 1 cocktail**

The girallon is one of the mightiest of the fantasy apes, resembling a massive white gorilla with an extra set of powerfully muscled arms just beneath the regular set, ready to pound, rip, tear, and dismember their foes. Curiously, the arms are also perfectly suited to hold a deliciously complex absinthe and gin cocktail in one hand while adroitly using the other three for sophisticated gesticulation at a formal soiree.

*1½ ounces gin*
*1½ ounces orange juice*
*1 teaspoon grenadine*
*1 teaspoon absinthe*
*2 banana slices*

1. Place a cocktail glass in the freezer, allowing it to chill as you prepare the drink.

2. Fill a cocktail shaker with ice. Add all ingredients except banana.

3. Shake and strain into chilled cocktail glass. Garnish with a banana slice, or you could spear banana slices on each end of a toothpick to create a tiny barbell and hang toothpick on rim as garnish.

> **DÜNGEONMEISTER TIP**
>
> Try not to four-hand these delicious beverages, instead stick to one or two cocktails to leave a hand free for the charcuterie board. The herbal citrus zing from the Girallon and On is perfectly paired with mellow soft cheeses and salty olives, or prosciutto cruelly torn from the hides of your mortal enemies.

CHAPTER 6: IMMENSE INTOXICANTS | 133

# Chapter 7

# METAGAME MADNESS

While using metagame knowledge is usually frowned upon, these drinks based on metagame terms are sure to bring smiles. Now when the GM is responsible for a TPK, you can thank them for the tasty beverage instead of quietly cursing them and plotting how you will eventually take revenge in a satisfying way. Oh, they'll rue the day. Oh, yes. Soon. Soon.

# Düngeonmeister

**Complexity: 1**  **Yields 1 shot**

When it comes time to proffer a drink to the one running your game, it's best to err on the side of something delicious that anyone could enjoy. This mix of liqueurs simulates a fresh cookie, in case you didn't have any homemade to give as an offering.

- ¾ ounce butterscotch schnapps
- ¾ ounce Irish cream liqueur
- ½ teaspoon Jägermeister
- ½ teaspoon cinnamon schnapps

Fill a cocktail shaker with ice. Add all ingredients. Shake and strain into a shot glass.

> **DÜNGEONMEISTER TIP**
>
> Oftentimes people will talk about pizza in relation to their GM—buying pizza, not touching the GM's pizza—all to try to bribe them. Perhaps the better way to butter up the Game Master is to get them sloshed and ask for that magic item you've been wanting.

# Horror Factor

**Complexity: 2**  **Yields 1 cocktail**

When determining just how spooky a monster is, there is a very scientific formula known as the horror factor that one can use. It considers the many aspects of a thing. For example, while this drink might seem spooky at first, it is actually fairly low on the horror factor due to its blend of creamy and tangy flavors. Also, because it is a drink.

- 2 ounces dark rum
- ½ cup heavy cream
- ½ ounce cinnamon simple syrup (see recipe in Tavern Basics)
- 1 large pasteurized egg white
- 2 ounces sparkling apple cider
- ⅛ teaspoon powdered activated charcoal

1. Add rum, cream, syrup, and egg white to a cocktail shaker (without ice). Shake vigorously for 30 seconds.
2. Add ice to the shaker and shake again to chill.
3. Strain into a coupe glass and slowly top with cider. Sprinkle activated charcoal over top.

> **DÜNGEONMEISTER TIP**
>
> If you can't find powdered activated charcoal, do not substitute for nonactivated charcoal. We cannot stress this enough. However, the ashes of a burned ghost should suffice. Don't use any other kind of ashes, though. You'll get so haunted.

# Fudge the Dice

**Complexity: 2**  **Yields 1 cocktail**

When you're on the brink of disaster and that crucial roll just won't happen, sometimes you need to fudge the roll a little. If you feel like you deserve a win, you can't go wrong with this chocolaty, decadent drink that's so good it feels like you're cheating.

*1 cup crushed ice*
*2 scoops chocolate ice cream*
*1 ounce chocolate syrup*
*1 ounce coffee liqueur*
*1 ounce crème de cacao*
*1 ounce vodka*
*1 tablespoon whipped cream*
*1 stemmed maraschino cherry*

1. Place all ingredients except whipped cream and cherry in a blender and blend until smooth, approximately 30 seconds.
2. Pour into a hurricane glass.
3. Garnish with whipped cream and cherry.

### DÜNGEONMEISTER TIP

The jury is out on whether fudging the dice is an acceptable practice. Some think it's never okay. Some say it's okay only for GMs to do it to save the party from random chance ruining things. Still others say that if your dice are made of fudge, then they aren't going to keep very well, and you should eat them immediately.

# The Level Up

**Complexity: 1**                                              **Yields 1 cocktail**

Players are going to feel like celebrating when they level up; it's just the nature of the game! When it happens, why not boost those festivities with a drink that's sunny, bright, and effervescent to boot? Give them a little taste of the good life, then start throwing monsters and traps at them again.

> ½ cup unsweetened shredded coconut
> 2 tablespoons simple syrup (see recipe in Tavern Basics) or honey
> 1½ ounces pineapple juice
> 1½ ounces coconut juice
> 2 ounces champagne or sparkling wine

1. Spread coconut in a shallow dish. Add syrup to a small bowl.

2. Dip the rim of a champagne flute in syrup, then dip the moistened rim in coconut to coat lightly and set aside to set (about 1 minute).

3. Add juices to flute, then top with champagne.

> **DÜNGEONMEISTER TIP**
>
> If you're still playing an old-school game at your table, one old enough to have level drain, you'd be well advised to avoid this drink, or at least provide a bucket.

# The Natural 20

**Complexity: 1**                                                  **Yields 1 cocktail**

Few moments are more worthy of celebration than the one when your die clatters to a halt on that magic number, 20. It's a crit! Savor the 5 percent chance of ultimate victory, which naturally is a blend of fruit and berry given complex life by the addition of a touch of the bittersweet. After all, your celebration song is some unfortunate monster's dirge.

- ¾ ounce citrus vodka
- ¾ ounce raspberry vodka
- ¾ ounce apple juice
- ¾ ounce lime juice
- ½ ounce simple syrup (*see recipe in Tavern Basics*)
- ¼ teaspoon aromatic bitters
- 2 fresh blackberries

1. Place a martini glass in the freezer, allowing it to chill as you prepare the drink.
2. Fill a cocktail shaker with ice. Add all ingredients except blackberries.
3. Shake and strain into chilled martini glass. Spear blackberries on a toothpick and hang toothpick on the rim as garnish.

# Never Split the Party Punch

**Complexity: 1**  **Yields 1 punch bowl (serves 6)**

Veteran players know that when you are faced with a problem, you should never split the party and instead face any threat as a unified team. This bubbly, sweet drink will make sure that everyone wants to gather together, and no rogues are tempted to go off by themselves.

*12 ounces melon liqueur*
*8 ounces vanilla vodka*
*4 ounces raspberry vodka*
*3 ounces pineapple juice*
*3 ounces club soda*
*12 slices fresh strawberry*

1. Fill a punch bowl halfway with ice. Add all ingredients except strawberry slices and stir with a bar spoon.

2. Serve in punch cups filled with ice. Garnish each drink with 2 strawberry slices.

### DÜNGEONMEISTER TIP

The secret to a good party punch is to keep an extra amount of all the ingredients separately, not only so that you can make more punch but so that individuals can add more of anything to their own drink to make it more to their liking. Now everybody in the party is happy. Except Dan. That guy's never happy. C'mon, Dan!

CHAPTER 7: METAGAME MADNESS | 145

# Session Zero

**Complexity: 1**                  **Yields 1 punch bowl (serves 12)**

Before really getting into the adventure, lots of groups have a Session Zero to establish things that they want out of the game. This refreshing and easy-to-make punch gets everybody around the table and talking to each other, the perfect start to the night.

*16 ounces vodka*
*16 ounces light rum*
*10 (12-ounce) cans Keystone Ice (or beer of your choice)*
*1 (12-ounce) can frozen lemonade concentrate*
*1 lemon, sliced into wheels*

1. Add all ingredients except lemon to a punch bowl.
2. Mix with a bar spoon and chill until serving.
3. Garnish punch cups with 1 lemon wheel each.

> **DÜNGEONMEISTER TIP**
>
> Sometimes people will skip the Session Zero and get right into the thick of it. While certainly a valid way of doing things, there is something to be said for making sure that you don't show up to the group with an Orc Barbarian and a fellow party member who is a Paladin of Hating Specifically Orcs.

# The TPK

**Complexity: 1**                                                            **Yields 1 cocktail**

TPK stands for Total Party Kill, which is the moment at which an encounter is too overwhelming and demolishes every character without a chance. It is brutal, it is sudden, and it will be regretted in the morning, thus the TPK. You'll need something this strong to wash defeat out of your mouth.

- ½ ounce vodka
- ½ ounce dark rum
- ½ ounce tequila
- ½ ounce gin
- ½ ounce blue curaçao
- 2 ounces sweet and sour mix (see recipe in Tavern Basics)
- 2 ounces lemon-lime soda
- 1 stemmed maraschino cherry

1. Fill a highball glass with ice. Add all ingredients except soda and cherry and stir with a bar spoon.
2. Top with soda and garnish with cherry.

> **DÜNGEONMEISTER TIP**
>
> When facing down the sad and inevitable doom of a TPK, try to remain calm. Make yourself comfortable as the crushing enormity of your failure crashes down around you. Just remember: It's all the GM's fault. If they didn't want you to attack that dragon, they shouldn't have given it so much treasure.

# Peek Behind the Screen

**Complexity: 1**  **Yields 1 cocktail**

What lies beyond the GM screen is one of the great mysteries players encounter in a good dungeon crawl. The secret of what's behind the screen: chaos. So, GM, you'll need a good drink packed with a funky herbaceous kick, to keep the players thinking you've got this all figured out.

- 1 ounce dry gin
- 1 ounce sweet vermouth
- 1 ounce green Chartreuse
- ⅛ teaspoon orange bitters
- 1 lemon twist (peel)

1. Place a cocktail glass in the freezer, allowing it to chill.
2. Fill a cocktail shaker with ice. Add all ingredients except lemon.
3. Shake and strain into chilled cocktail glass.
4. Twist lemon peel over glass to express oils, then add as garnish.

> **DÜNGEONMEISTER TIP**
>
> FOR GM EYES ONLY: Okay GMs, we know the bitterness you actually keep hidden behind the screen. It's the same flavor as in this drink. Sour bitterness that you inflict on your players. Enjoy the drink; you've earned it.

# Chapter 8

## ALCOHOLIC ARTIFACTS

Finally, it's time for the one thing that really matters. The loot. The goods. The piles and piles of treasure that you worked so hard to get. Make sure none of these items are too powerful, or it could unbalance your game. If you're unsure if the game is balanced, have your players walk a straight line while touching their nose and reciting the alphabet backward.

# Treasure Type J

**Complexity: 1**                                                  **Yields 1 cocktail**

The hard-earned reward for slaying a particularly challenging dragon, the Treasure Type J is a hoard indeed, gold shot through with yet more gold. A spicy-sweet taste of the glories that keep your party venturing into mortal danger, this cocktail is an exceptional celebration for an adventure well played.

- ½ ounce Goldschläger
- ½ ounce lemon juice
- 3 ounces chilled sparkling wine (brut preferred)
- ¼ teaspoon orange bitters

1. Pour Goldschläger and lemon juice into a champagne glass.
2. Add sparkling wine and bitters. Stir gently with a bar spoon.

> **DÜNGEONMEISTER TIP**
>
> The actual Treasure Type J is mostly the garbage left behind when a giant spider eats a bunch of farmers, and their scattered tools and copper pieces rain to the sodden cave floor below. Creative license has been applied here, as Treasure Type H, the huge mountains of gold on which dragons slumber, has a worse ring to it. No one wants to drink an H.

# Astral Diamond Juice

**Complexity: 2**  **Yields 1 cocktail**

The astral diamond is the ultimate currency. Worth thousands of gold pieces, unheard of by the common folk, and draped in beauty hitherto unspoken, these gems are the coin of the realm for the most powerful wizards, the most opulent demigods, and the most mythical merchants. In this recipe, we teach you how to squeeze this diamond and drink what comes out of there.

¾ ounce Hendrick's gin
¾ ounce crème de violette
¼ ounce blue curaçao
1 lemon wedge
3 ounces champagne or sparkling wine
1 teaspoon silver luster dust

1. Fill a mixing glass with ice. Add gin, crème de violette, and curaçao.
2. Squeeze lemon wedge into glass and discard the peel.
3. Stir with a bar spoon and strain into a champagne flute.
4. Top with champagne and sprinkle with luster dust.

> **DÜNGEONMEISTER TIP**
>
> Though for most mortals the astral diamond is little more than a myth, that's no excuse not to flaunt one if you have it. Once you've crafted this cocktail, be conspicuous about it. And don't share it with anyone without an exchange of at least a Sun Blade or Vorpal sword.

# Electrum Piece

**Complexity: 2**  **Yields 1 shot**

The rare electrum piece is minted from an alloy of gold and silver and is worth five silver pieces. Despite being half the value of a gold piece, they have a reputation in many fantasy circles akin to the two-dollar bill in that they're worth two dollars unless you're someone's weird uncle, at which point they become priceless. As a shot, this "piece" combines gold and silver in an alloy of explosive flavor that will entertain much more than any weird uncle.

¾ ounce Goldschläger
¾ ounce energy drink
Smidgen silver luster dust

1. Pour Goldschläger and energy drink into a shot glass.
2. Add luster dust and stir with a swizzle stick.

> **DÜNGEONMEISTER TIP**
>
> Dragons are known to hoard the electrum piece from time to time when forming their mighty piles to defend. This could be for a variety of reasons, from availability of gold to magical preference. Most commonly, however, it is held up as evidence that even dragons can be weird uncles.

CHAPTER 8: ALCOHOLIC ARTIFACTS | 155

# Magic Mirror

**Complexity: 2**                                      **Yields 2 cocktails**

Magic mirrors are versatile artifacts that can let you see other places or future events, or even discern a metric of standard beauty by which one could judge someone against another. Whatever you see in this glimmering cocktail, you can be sure that the sweet flavor and unique look will make this the fairest in the land.

*3 ounces light rum*
*3 ounces blue curaçao*
*½ ounce grenadine*
*1 teaspoon silver luster dust, divided*
*2 lemon twists (peels)*

1. Fill a cocktail shaker with ice. Add rum, curaçao, and grenadine.

2. Shake and strain into two cocktail glasses.

3. Add ½ teaspoon luster dust to each glass and stir to dissolve. Garnish each glass with a lemon twist.

> **DÜNGEONMEISTER TIP**
>
> For most people, a magic mirror is one of the most important assets you could have. You can gain intel on enemy movements, spy on rival kingdoms, and see into a possible future for your endeavors. Judging a beauty contest is probably the least useful thing you could do with one.

# Potion of Glibness

**Complexity: 1**  **Yields 1 cocktail**

Some people just don't have the gift of gab. Others merely want to improve their already decent social talents. Whatever the reason, many an adventurer has turned to a Potion of Glibness. With a sour and smooth flavor, this particular potion is sure to loosen up your lips and get the words flowing.

- ½ cup lemonade
- 2 ounces cran-raspberry juice
- ⅕ ounce light rum
- 2 tablespoons lime juice

Fill a cocktail shaker with ice. Add all ingredients. Shake and strain into a cocktail glass.

> **DÜNGEONMEISTER TIP**
>
> Nothing is worse than when you're chatting up everyone and being the life of the party and suddenly your Potion of Glibness wears off. What to do? This simple incantation can get you out of there without anyone the wiser. Verbal Component: "Wow, look at the time!" Somatic Component: Going home.

# Epic Upgrade

**Complexity: 3**　　　　　　　　　　　　　　　**Yields 1 cocktail**

No one is sure when we started to accept as a society that blue is exceptional, but purple is epic. If you're looking for an impressive beverage upgrade, this cocktail, which near-miraculously shifts from blue to purple, is the way to do it. The secret lies in rapid pH alteration of the pea flower tea, so keep your flask of citric acid water handy to instantly shift this beverage from a gin and tea to a gin and lemon.

For the Butterfly Pea Flower Tea:
3 grams dried butterfly pea flowers
1 cup hot water

For the Cocktail:
½ teaspoon citric acid
6 tablespoons water
2 ounces gin
¾ ounce simple syrup (see recipe in Tavern Basics)
1 ounce Butterfly Pea Flower Tea

1. For the Butterfly Pea Flower Tea: Add flowers to water and steep until very dark blue, at least 5–7 minutes. Strain the liquid into another container to remove flowers.

2. For the Cocktail: Combine citric acid and water in a small cup and stir to combine, then pour into a shot glass.

3. Fill a cocktail shaker with ice. Add gin, syrup, and tea. Shake and strain into a martini glass.

4. When ready to serve, pour citric acid mixture into cocktail glass and watch the cocktail change color.

# Pool of Radiance

**Complexity: 2**　　　　　　　　　　**Yields 1 punch bowl (serves 8)**

Planning a spooky party or an extended dungeon run? This playful punch can add a touch of magic and mysticism to your snack table. You'll need a black light on hand, and when it's switched on, you'll be presented with a glowing beverage. The secret is the fluorescing quinine in tonic water, which lends the drink its distinctive bitterness. We battle that bitterness with pineapple, lime, and orange flavors, resulting in a magical phial of glowing goodness.

*For the Ice Cubes:*
3 cups flat tonic water
*For the Cocktail:*
24 ounces pisco
12 ounces Cointreau
12 ounces lime juice
12 ounces pineapple juice
7 cups tonic water

1. For the Ice Cubes: Fill ice cube trays with flat tonic water and put in the freezer 24 hours in advance.

2. For the Cocktail: Add pisco, Cointreau, and juices to a large container and stir with a bar spoon. Refrigerate until ready to serve.

3. Add juice mixture to a punch bowl and add tonic water, stirring gently with a bar spoon to combine.

4. Add Ice Cubes and serve in punch cups under black light.

CHAPTER 8: ALCOHOLIC ARTIFACTS

# Potion of Strength

**Complexity: 1**  **Yields 2 cocktails**

While a practiced hand and a trained body cannot be replaced with a mere potion, those wishing to give themselves the alchemical edge over their opponent will turn to potions. This bubbling dark elixir appears murky at first but hides a powerful sweetness within.

- 8 ounces pomegranate juice
- 3 ounces strawberry vodka
- 3 ounces black raspberry liqueur

1. Place two martini glasses in the freezer, allowing them to chill as you prepare the drink.
2. Fill a cocktail shaker with ice. Add all ingredients. Shake and strain into chilled martini glasses.

> **DÜNGEONMEISTER TIP**
>
> If you're going into battle and you need to be at your strongest, this is the potion for you. You may even find that the potion is too strong for you, and you will have to travel to a potion seller who sells weaker potions. If such is the case, make sure that they have respect for knights such as yourself.

# Golden Hoard

**Complexity: 1**  **Yields 1 cocktail**

Liquid gold, that's what you're seeing here, a complex cocktail with a wealth of deep flavors and sweet citrus scents. The true treasure at the end of the dungeon, whether you enjoy it in the mad king's booby-trapped castle or in the tavern once you're done divvying up the spoils. Congratulations, you've acquired the hoard, and you don't have to share it with anyone else. You can almost afford full plate armor now.

2 tablespoons granulated sugar
1 lime wedge
1½ ounces gin
¾ ounce dry vermouth
¾ ounce sweet vermouth
¾ ounce orange juice
¼ teaspoon bitters

1. Place a cocktail glass in the freezer, allowing it to chill as you prepare the drink.

2. Spread sugar in a shallow dish. Use 1 lime wedge to moisten the rim of the cocktail glass, then dip the moistened rim into sugar to coat lightly.

3. Fill a cocktail shaker with ice. Add gin, vermouths, juice, and bitters.

4. Shake and strain into chilled cocktail glass.

CHAPTER 8: ALCOHOLIC ARTIFACTS | 165

# Chapter 9

## PHANTOM FLUIDS

Glittering shimmers, bursts of flavor that seem so exotic that you're tempted to roll to disbelieve them, and colors that seem pulled directly from the overactive imagination of a puissant illusionist mark the delights to be found within this fun chapter of concoctions. Focusing on illusory magics that fool the senses, these drinks may not be especially moored in reality, but their palate-pleasing complex flavors (and their refreshing alcohol-free simplicity) are certainly real enough. Let us weave you a series of magical delights so tantalizingly close to tangle you can almost taste them. Then, you know, go make them, so you can actually taste them.

# Color Spray

**Complexity: 2**  **Yields 4 mocktails**

A dazzling array of color rapidly shifting between yellows, purples, and blues, this beverage provides a more complex flavor profile than lemonade thanks to the earthy, slightly bitter pea flower tea. Thankfully, unlike the spell, your sight should remain unblurred with this mystical delight.

For the Butterfly Pea
  Flower Tea:
4 grams dried butterfly pea
  flowers
2 cups hot water

For the Mocktail:
2 cups Butterfly Pea Flower
  Tea ice cubes
2 cups lemonade

1. For the Butterfly Pea Flower Tea: Add flowers to water and steep until very dark blue, at least 5–7 minutes. Strain the liquid into another container to remove flowers, then pour into an ice cube tray. Freeze tea until completely solid.

2. For the Mocktail: Place frozen tea cubes in a blender and pulse until fully crushed.

3. Pour ½ cup blended ice and ½ cup lemonade into each glass. Serve.

> **DÜNGEONMEISTER TIP**
>
> Unlike the spell, we advise against hurling this beverage into an approaching enemy's face. Unless they insulted your friend at the garden party, in which case let fly, because this drink may be illusory, but you're keeping it real.

# Hallucinatory Garden Terrain

**Complexity: 1**　　　　　　　　　　　　　　　　　**Yields 1 mocktail**

Sweet, earthy, herby and fresh, this beverage packs a punch of flavor, even if it might not be real, just like the illusory enchanted gardens of its namesake. The rosemary simple syrup is a delicious complement to this fruity and tart drink.

>   2 ounces rosemary simple syrup (see recipe in Tavern Basics)
>   3 ounces pomegranate juice
>   3 ounces club soda

Fill a highball glass with ice. Add all ingredients and stir.

> **DÜNGEONMEISTER TIP**
>
> Hallucinatory gardens are an excellent source of imaginary herbs, succulent (nonexistent) tomatoes, and white rabbits with waistcoats and pocket watches. As a useful bonus, illusions are not drinkable, so you can't spill them on yourself. (Consult with your cleric or any available druid regarding your illusory needs.)

# Black Magic Mirror

**Complexity: 1**  **Yields 1 mocktail**

Mirror, mirror, how did you come to be so startlingly black and opaque? Maybe it's because this is the illusions chapter, and illusionists hate mirrors—they give the game away! In this concoction, you combine blackberries, pineapple juice, and blue curaçao syrup to produce a beverage as black as night. You'll simply have to try one to see how good these are; drinking is believing (and Perception checks are disbelieving).

*11 fresh blackberries, divided*
*4 ounces canned pineapple juice*
*1 ounce blue curaçao syrup*
*3 ounces gin alternative*

1. Place 10 blackberries in a cocktail shaker and muddle until juice is released.

2. Add pineapple juice, curaçao syrup, and gin alternative, then fill the shaker with ice. Shake and strain into a coupe glass. Garnish with remaining blackberry.

> **DÜNGEONMEISTER TIP**
>
> Magical Mishap Warning: If your magic mirror develops a ghostly face that advises you to poison your attractive relatives, this could be the outside influence of a dark wizard or a bromelain enzyme imbalance. Consider swapping the canned pineapple juice for fresh and readying a scroll of Dispel Magic.

# SimulacRum Punch

**Complexity: 1**                                                                      **Yields 1 mocktail**

Magic can help you do a great many things including creating duplicates that are almost, but not quite, identical to the original. This punch has all the look and flavor of the quintessential summertime drink, but the replication process has drained the drink of all the alcohol. Be forewarned: This copy might just replace the original in your favorites!

- 3 ounces rum alternative
- 1½ ounces orange juice
- 1½ ounces pineapple juice
- 1 ounce lime juice
- 1 tablespoon grenadine
- 1 orange wheel
- 3 (or more) stemmed maraschino cherries

1. Fill a highball glass with ice. Add rum alternative, juices, and grenadine and stir.
2. Garnish with orange wheel and cherries.

> **DÜNGEONMEISTER TIP**
>
> For *true* cherry lovers, the number of cherries your heart desires is incalculable. If you have such an adoration, then try to limit your garnish to a light sprinkling of three to five cherries. This may be a pale shadow of the insatiable cherry lust within you, but think of the children!

CHAPTER 9: PHANTOM FLUIDS | 173

# Banana Balhannoth

**Complexity: 2**  **Yields 2 mocktails**

The Balhannoth is a creature of the Underdark that can sense what it is that you desire most and make you begin to imagine that their lair holds that thing. Luckily, if what you most desire is a delicious banana-forward mocktail, then this is definitely not an illusionary trap—just ignore those tentacles.

- 1 banana, sliced
- ½ cup light coconut milk
- 1½ tablespoons lime juice
- 2 tablespoons maple syrup
- ½ cup seltzer
- 2 tablespoons unsweetened shredded coconut

1. Place banana, coconut milk, lime juice, syrup, and 3 ice cubes in a blender and blend until smooth, approximately 30 seconds.
2. Fill two highball glasses with ice. Add half of the blended drink to each glass and top with seltzer.
3. Garnish with shredded coconut.

> **DÜNGEONMEISTER TIP**
>
> Did I say tentacles? Those aren't tentacles. Those are bananas! Bananas from the banana drink we'll be having. It's an old family recipe for delicious mocktails. Now just close your eyes and step right into this welcoming maw of a kitchen.

# Magic Mouth

**Complexity: 2**  **Yields 1 mocktail**

When your friends taste this drink, it will be like you used this sweet, floral beverage to cast the illusion of Magic Mouth on them to deliver a message. And the message they will all be delivering is, "I can't believe how good this tastes!"

- 2 tablespoons plus ½ teaspoon granulated sugar, divided
- 1 lime wedge
- 3 ounces hibiscus tea
- 1 ounce orange juice
- ½ teaspoon rose water
- 2 ounces nonalcoholic rosé (still or sparkling)
- 1 pair of wax lips

1. Prepare the hibiscus tea according to packet instructions but with double the recommended amount of tea to water.

2. While tea is still warm, add ½ teaspoon sugar and stir. Then refrigerate to chill.

3. Spread remaining 2 tablespoons sugar in a shallow dish. Use 1 lime wedge to moisten the rim of the cocktail glass, then dip the moistened rim into sugar to coat lightly.

4. Fill a wine glass with ice and add tea and orange juice.

5. Add rose water and top with nonalcoholic rosé.

6. Stir gently and place wax lips in the glass.

# Coupe of Elvenkind

**Complexity: 1**  **Yields 1 mocktail**

The items of Elvenkind are known to allow the users to blend into their surroundings more easily. With this nonalcoholic take on an amaretto sour, you'll be sure to stealth your way past even the most discerning of taste buds without any complaints.

1½ ounces nonalcoholic aperitif
1 ounce lemon juice
¼ ounce orgeat
¼ ounce apricot preserves (or any stone fruit jam)
1 large pasteurized egg white
1 lemon twist (peel)

1. Place a coupe glass in the freezer, allowing it to chill as you prepare the drink.

2. In a cocktail shaker, add nonalcoholic aperitif, lemon juice, orgeat, preserves, and egg white. Dry shake without ice to structure the foam.

3. Add large ice cubes to the shaker. Shake and strain into chilled coupe glass. Garnish with lemon twist.

> **DÜNGEONMEISTER TIP**
>
> This is not to be mistaken with the other Coupe of Elvenkind, which is a two-door sports car that lets you blend into traffic and no matter how fast you're going, the cops won't be able to pick you out.

# Invisibilitea

**Complexity: 2**                                                                 **Yields 2 mocktails**

Adventurers love the bright and citrusy flavor of this refreshing mocktail, but can they see what gives it such complexity and body? No, they cannot because they literally can't see this drink at all—the whole invisibility aspect of the drink, and all. It's the white tea, though.

- 6 ounces white tea
- 1 teaspoon granulated sugar
- 1 grapefruit, juiced and zested
- 2 tablespoons fine grain sea salt (or kosher salt)
- 2 tablespoons honey
- 4 ounces lime juice
- 12 ounces grapefruit sparkling water

1. Prepare the white tea using two teabags for 8 ounces of boiling water.
2. While tea is still warm, add sugar and stir. Then refrigerate to chill.
3. In a shallow dish, mix grapefruit zest with salt. In another small dish, spread honey.
4. Dip the rims of two highball glasses in honey, then dip the moistened rims into zest mixture to coat lightly. Fill both glasses with ice.
5. Fill a cocktail shaker with ice. Add grapefruit juice, lime juice, and tea.
6. Shake and strain mixture into prepared glasses. Top with sparkling water.

# Ranch Water Weird

**Complexity: 1**                                              **Yields 1 mocktail**

The Water Weird is an especially powerful form of illusion magic, calling up what seem to be malicious water elementals in the form of great snakes or tentacles to bash the foes of the caster into soaking pieces. Even if the weirds were never real, the experience is so intense that it can cause real damage to those who believe they were. We've added a cowboy hat and some lime juice so that when you're smashing your enemies flat, at least they exit the scene and the material plane feeling refreshed and zesty.

2 ounces tequila alternative
1½ limes, juiced
½ ounce simple syrup (see recipe in Tavern Basics)

6 ounces sparkling water
1 lime wedge

1. Fill a Collins glass with ice. Add tequila alternative and lime juice.

2. Add syrup, top with sparkling water, and stir.

3. Garnish with lime wedge.

> **DÜNGEONMEISTER TIP**
>
> For an even more refreshing alternative, try the Ranch Water Normal, which is just a glass of water that doesn't do anything or have any complex ingredients. It's not even illusory, but you should try to consume several full glasses of it a day for your health, according to leading illusionary doctors.

# Blur Berry

**Complexity: 1**                                                          **Yields 1 mocktail**

This berry-infused take on a classic sour will blur the lines between mocktail and cocktail such that nobody will be able to tell where it actually stands. With no alcohol, though, you won't have to worry about things getting blurry on your end.

- 1 cup fresh blueberries
- 2 ounces lemon juice
- 1 ounce simple syrup (see recipe in Tavern Basics)
- 2 ounces gin alternative
- ¼ teaspoon aromatic bitters
- 1 large pasteurized egg white
- 1 lemon wheel

1. Place blueberries, lemon juice, and syrup in a cocktail shaker and muddle.

2. Add gin alternative, bitters, and egg white and shake until frothy.

3. Add ice and shake for a few more seconds. Strain into a rocks glass filled with ice. Garnish with lemon wheel.

### DÜNGEONMEISTER TIP

The blur berry is itself a magical fruit that is very hard to find. You might think that it is hard to find because of the whole "blur" thing and that it ends up not being where you think it is. And you would be right, but it's also hard to find because it only grows in illusory terrain, making it doubly difficult to get to.

# US/Metric Conversion Chart

## VOLUME CONVERSIONS

| US VOLUME MEASURE | METRIC EQUIVALENT |
|---|---|
| ⅛ teaspoon | 0.5 milliliter |
| ¼ teaspoon | 1 milliliter |
| ½ teaspoon | 2 milliliters |
| 1 teaspoon | 5 milliliters |
| ½ tablespoon | 7 milliliters |
| 1 tablespoon (3 teaspoons) | 15 milliliters |
| 2 tablespoons (1 fluid ounce) | 30 milliliters |
| ¼ cup (4 tablespoons) | 60 milliliters |
| ⅓ cup | 90 milliliters |
| ½ cup (4 fluid ounces) | 125 milliliters |
| ⅔ cup | 160 milliliters |
| ¾ cup (6 fluid ounces) | 180 milliliters |
| 1 cup (16 tablespoons) | 250 milliliters |
| 1 pint (2 cups) | 500 milliliters |
| 1 quart (4 cups) | 1 liter (about) |

## WEIGHT CONVERSIONS

| US VOLUME MEASURE | METRIC EQUIVALENT |
| --- | --- |
| ½ ounce | 15 grams |
| 1 ounce | 30 grams |
| 2 ounces | 60 grams |
| 3 ounces | 85 grams |
| ¼ pound (4 ounces) | 115 grams |
| ½ pound (8 ounces) | 225 grams |
| ¾ pound (12 ounces) | 340 grams |
| 1 pound (16 ounces) | 454 grams |

## OVEN TEMPERATURE CONVERSIONS

| DEGREES FAHRENHEIT | DEGREES CELSIUS |
| --- | --- |
| 200 degrees F | 95 degrees C |
| 250 degrees F | 120 degrees C |
| 275 degrees F | 135 degrees C |
| 300 degrees F | 150 degrees C |
| 325 degrees F | 160 degrees C |
| 350 degrees F | 180 degrees C |
| 375 degrees F | 190 degrees C |
| 400 degrees F | 205 degrees C |
| 425 degrees F | 220 degrees C |
| 450 degrees F | 230 degrees C |

# INDEX

Aasimartini, 31
Acid Arrow, 75
Alcohol-free drinks, modifying recipes for, 16–17. *See also* Phantom fluids (mocktails)
Alcoholic artifacts, **151**–66
    Astral Diamond Juice, 153
    Electrum Piece, 154
    Epic Upgrade, 159
    Golden Hoard, 164
    Magic Mirror, 156
    Pool of Radiance, 160
    Potion of Glibness, 157
    Potion of Strength, 163
    Treasure Type J, 152
Amaretto
    Barbarian Rage, 43
    Power Attack, 64
    Royal Diplomacy, 65
    Seduction Roll, 63
Aperitif (nonalcoholic), mocktail with, 178
Aperol, in Gin and Skeletonic, 114
Astral Diamond Juice, 153

Banana Balhannoth, 175
Barbarian Rage, 43
Bard's Songs, 44
Bar tools, 20
Beer
    Claw Claw Snakebite, 123
    Coors Light Wounds, 76
    Session Zero, 146
Berries
    Black Magic Mirror (mocktail), 171
    Blur Berry, 182
    Goodberries (with Goodberry Syrup), 96
    Goodberry Syrup, 17–18
    Spiced Berry Coulis, 29
Black Magic Mirror, 171
Black Mana, 78
Black raspberry liqueur. *See* Raspberry liqueur
Blue curaçao
    Astral Diamond Juice, 153
    Barbarian Rage, 43
    Blue Mana, 84
    Faerie Fire, 82
    Magic Mirror, 156
    Mermaid Lagoon, 109
    Psionic Blasts, 92
    Purple Worm, 128
    Release the Kraken, 131
    The TPK (Total Party Kill), 147

Blue Mana, 84
Blur Berry, 182
Bourbon
    1d3 Wandering Minstrels, 106
    Power Attack, 64
    Tiefling's Breakfast, 35
Breath Weapon, 120
Butterfly Pea Flower Tea, 159
Butterscotch schnapps
    Düngeonmeister, 137
    Slippery Grippli, 37

Campari, in Gnomish Gnightcap, 26
Champagne or sparkling wine
    Astral Diamond Juice, 153
    Bard's Songs, 44
    The Level Up, 141
    Magic Moth (mocktail), 176
    Mermaid Lagoon, 109
    Treasure Type J, 152
Chartreuse, in Peek Behind the Screen, 149
Cherry liqueur, in Sweet and Sour-cerer, 52
Cider
    Cinnamon Cider (in Stunning Smite), 51
    Claw Claw Snakebite, 123
    Horror Factor, 138
Cinnamon Cider, 51
Citric acid, 19
Class-y drinks, **41**–56
    Barbarian Rage, 43
    Bard's Songs, 44
    Flavored Enemy, 46
    Gnomish Illusionist, 55
    Holy Water, 47
    Necromancer, 49
    Sneak Attack, 50
    Stunning Smite, 51
    Sweet and Sour-cerer, 52

Sword and Chambord, 56
Claw Claw Snakebite, 123
Coffee liqueur
    Black Mana, 78
    Fudge the Dice, 140
    Turn Undead, 69
    Wight Russian, 113
Cognac, in Hpnotiq Pattern, 83
Cointreau
    Necromancer, 49
    Pool of Radiance, 160
    Power Attack, 64
    Sneak Attack, 50
Color Spray, 169
Complexity rating, about, 12
Coors Light Wounds, 76
Coupe of Elvenkind, 178
Crème de cacao liqueur
    Black Mana, 78
    Fudge the Dice, 140
    Half 'n' Half-Orc, 32
Crème de menthe, in Half 'n' Half-Orc, 32
Crème de violette, in Astral Diamond Juice, 153

Dark Elf, 25
Dragon the Beach, 125
Drambuie, in Rust Monster, 116
Düngeonmeister, 137
Dwarven Forge, 29–30

Elderflower liqueur
    Holy Water, 47
    Mai Tyrant, 126
    Pixie Dust, 17–18
Electrum Piece, 154
Elemental Plane of Fire, 77
Epic Upgrade, 159

Escape Artist, 60

Faerie Fire, 82
Flavored Enemy, 46
Fudge the Dice, 140

Gelatinous Cubes, 98
Giant Bee, 101
Gin
   about: types of, 14
   Astral Diamond Juice, 153
   Barbarian Rage, 43
   Bard's Songs, 44
   Black Magic Mirror (mocktail), 171
   Epic Upgrade, 159
   Faerie Fire, 82
   Giant Bee, 101
   Gin and Skeletonic, 114
   Girallon and On, 131
   Gnomish Gnightcap, 26
   Golden Hoard, 164
   Magic Mistletoe, 91
   Necromancer, 49
   Peek Behind the Screen, 149
   Point Blank Shot, 61
   Power Attack, 64
   Silver Dragon, 129
   Stealth Checks, 66
   The TPK (Total Party Kill), 147
Ginger beer, in Sword and Chambord, 56
Girallon and On, 131
Glassware, 20
Glitter, edible (luster dust), 19
Gnomish Gnightcap, 26
Gnomish Illusionist, 55
Goblin Grenades, 102–3
Golden Hoard, 164
Goldschläger

Electrum Piece, 154
Gelatinous Cubes, 98
Treasure Type J, 152
Goodberries, 96
Goodberry Syrup, 17–18
Green Mana, 81

Halflings, 22
Half 'n' Half-Orc, 32
Hallucinatory Garden Terrain, 170
Healing Surge, 58
Honey syrup, 18
Horror Factor, 138
Hpnotiq Pattern, 83

Illithid Substance, 104
Immense intoxicants, **117**–33
   Breath Weapon, 120
   Claw Claw Snakebite, 123
   Dragon the Beach, 125
   Girallon and On, 131
   Mai Tyrant, 126
   Nature Goddess, 122
   Purple Worm, 128
   Release the Kraken, 131
   Silver Dragon, 129
   The 666 Layers of the Abyss, Now with Coconut, 119
Invisibilitea, 179
Irish cream liqueur
   Aasimartini, 31
   Düngeonmeister, 137
   Gnomish Illusionist, 55
   Slippery Grippli, 37

Jägermeister
   Acid Arrow, 75
   Düngeonmeister, 137

Kobold Fashioned, 107

Lemon vodka. See Vodka, citrus/lemon
The Level Up, 141
Luster dust, 19

Magic Mirror, 156
Magic Mistletoe, 91
Magic mixers, **73**–96
    Acid Arrow, 75
    Black Mana, 78
    Blue Mana, 84
    Coors Light Wounds, 76
    Elemental Plane of Fire, 77
    Faerie Fire, 82
    Goodberries, 96
    Green Mana, 81
    Hpnotiq Pattern, 83
    Magic Mistletoe, 91
    Peanut Butter & Jellikinesis, 95
    Psionic Blasts, 92
    Red Mana, 87
    White Mana, 88
Magic Mouth, 176
Mai Tyrant, 126
Maraschino liqueur, in Sneak Attack, 50
Melon liqueur
    Barbarian Rage, 43
    Green Mana, 81
    Mermaid Lagoon, 109
    Never Split the Party Punch, 144
    Slippery Grippli, 37
Mermaid Lagoon, 109
Metagame madness, **135**–49
    Düngeonmeister, 137
    Fudge the Dice, 140
    Horror Factor, 138
    The Level Up, 141

The Natural 20, 143
Never Split the Party Punch, 144
Peek Behind the Screen, 149
Session Zero, 146
The TPK (Total Party Kill), 147
Metric measurement conversion charts, 183–84
Mezcal, in Rust Monster, 116
Mixers, common, 17–19
Mocktails. See Phantom fluids (mocktails)
Muddled minions, **97**–116
    Gelatinous Cubes, 98
    Giant Bee, 101
    Gin and Skeletonic, 114
    Goblin Grenades, 102–3
    Illithid Substance, 104
    Kobold Fashioned, 107
    Mermaid Lagoon, 109
    1d3 Wandering Minstrels, 106
    Rust Monster, 116
    Troll Slobber, 110
    Wight Russian, 113

The Natural 20, 143
Nature Goddess, 122
Necromancer, 49
Never Split the Party Punch, 144
Non-alcoholic drinks, modifying recipes for, 16–17. See also Phantom fluids (mocktails)

1d3 Wandering Minstrels, 106

Peach schnapps
    Dark Elf, 25
    Dragon the Beach, 125
    Sprite of Hand, 70
Peanut Butter & Jellikinesis, 95
Peek Behind the Screen, 149

Phantom fluids (mocktails), **167**–82
    Banana Balhannoth, 175
    Black Magic Mirror, 171
    Blur Berry, 182
    Color Spray, 169
    Coupe of Elvenkind, 178
    Hallucinatory Garden Terrain, 170
    Invisibilitea, 179
    Magic Mouth, 176
    Ranch Water Weird (mocktail), 181
    SimulacRum Punch, 172
Pimm's No. 1 Cup, in Bard's Songs, 44
Pisco, in Pool of Radiance, 160
Pixie Dust, 38
Point Blank Shot, 61
Pool of Radiance, 160
Potion of Glibness, 157
Potion of Strength, 163
Power Attack, 64
Prosecco. *See* Champagne or sparkling wine
Psionic Blasts, 92
Purple Worm, 128

Ranch Water Weird, 181
Raspberry liqueur
    Barbarian Rage, 43
    Potion of Strength, 163
    Sword and Chambord, 56
Recipes
    complexity rating, 12
    modifying for alcohol-free drinks, 16–17
    this book and, 11–12
Red Mana, 87
Release the Kraken, 131
Rosemary Syrup, 17
Royal Diplomacy, 65
Rum. *See also specific flavors below*
    about, 15

Acid Arrow, 75
Mai Tyrant, 126
Rum, coconut, in Barbarian Rage, 43
Rum, dark
    Horror Factor, 138
    Release the Kraken, 131
    Three Halflings in a Trench Coat, 22
    The TPK (Total Party Kill), 147
Rum, overproof, in Dwarven Forge, 29–30
Rum, pineapple, in Troll Slobber, 110
Rum, silver
    Potion of Glibness, 157
    Session Zero, 146
Rum, spiced
    Barbarian Rage, 43
    Dwarven Forge, 29–30
Rum, white/light
    Barbarian Rage, 43
    Dark Elf, 25
    Green Mana, 81
    Magic Mirror, 156
    Mermaid Lagoon, 109
    SimulacRum Punch (mocktail), 172
    The 666 Layers of the Abyss, Now with Coconut, 119
    Sneak Attack, 50
    Sweet and Sour-cerer, 52
    Three Halflings in a Trench Coat, 22
Rust Monster, 116
Rye whiskey, in Kobold Fashioned, 107

Seduction Roll, 63
Session Zero, 146
Silver Dragon, 129
Simple syrup, 17
SimulacRum Punch, 172
The 666 Layers of the Abyss, Now with Coconut, 119

Skilled selections, **57**–72
    Escape Artist, 60
    Healing Surge, 58
    Point Blank Shot, 61
    Power Attack, 64
    Royal Diplomacy, 65
    Seduction Roll, 63
    Sprite of Hand, 70
    Stealth Checks, 66
    Turn Undead, 69
    Twin Strikes, 72
Sleep Immunity, 34
Slippery Grippli, 37
Sneak Attack, 50
Sour apple liqueur
    Healing Surge, 58
    Illithid Substance, 104
Southern Comfort
    Power Attack, 64
    Royal Diplomacy, 65
Sparkling wine. *See* Champagne or sparkling wine
Species. *See* Spirited species
Spiced Berry Coulis, 29
Spirited species, **21**–39
    Aasimartini, 31
    Dark Elf, 25
    Dwarven Forge, 29–30
    Gnomish Gnightcap, 26
    Half 'n' Half-Orc, 32
    Pixie Dust, 17–18
    Sleep Immunity, 34
    Slippery Grippli, 37
    Three Halflings in a Trench Coat, 22
    Tiefling's Breakfast, 35
Sprite of Hand, 70
Stealth Checks, 66
Stunning Smite, 51

Sweet and Sour-cerer, 52
Sweet and sour mix, 19
Sword and Chambord, 56
Syrups
    about: complex syrup, 18; honey syrup, 18; simple syrup, 17
    Goodberry Syrup, 17–18
    Grape Jelly Simple Syrup, 18
    Rosemary Syrup, 17

Taverns
    about: basics overview, 13
    bar tools, 20
    essential spirits to stock, 14–15
    mixers to have, 17–19
Tea
    Butterfly Pea Flower Tea, 159, 169
    Color Spray (mocktail with white tea), 169
    Invisibilitea (mocktail), 179
    Magic Mouth (mocktail with hibiscus tea), 176
Tequila
    about, 15
    Barbarian Rage, 43
    Elemental Plane of Fire, 77
    Goodberries, 96
    Healing Surge, 58
    Holy Water, 47
    Ranch Water Weird (mocktail), 181
    The TPK (Total Party Kill), 147
Three Halflings in a Trench Coat, 22
Tiefling's Breakfast, 35
Tools, bar, 20
The TPK (Total Party Kill), 147
Treasure Type J, 152
Triple sec, in Twin Strikes, 72
Troll Slobber, 110

Turn Undead, 69
Twin Strikes, 72

Vermouth, dry
  Breath Weapon, 120
  Escape Artist, 60
  Golden Hoard, 164
Vermouth, sweet
  Faerie Fire, 82
  Gnomish Gnightcap, 26
  Golden Hoard, 164
  Peek Behind the Screen, 149
Vodka. *See also specific flavors below*
  Aasimartini, 31
  about, 14
  Barbarian Rage, 43
  Blue Mana, 84
  Breath Weapon, 120
  Dragon the Beach, 125
  Escape Artist, 60
  Fudge the Dice, 140
  Gnomish Illusionist, 55
  Nature Goddess, 122
  Pixie Dust, 17–18
  Psionic Blasts, 92
  Purple Worm, 128
  Seduction Roll, 63
  Session Zero, 146
  Sleep Immunity, 34
  Sword and Chambord, 56
  The TPK (Total Party Kill), 147
  Turn Undead, 69
  Twin Strikes, 72
Vodka, chocolate, in White Mana, 88
Vodka, citrus/lemon
  Blue Mana, 84
  Goblin Grenades, 102–3
  The Natural 20, 143

Vodka, raspberry
  The Natural 20, 143
  Never Split the Party Punch, 144
Vodka, strawberry, in Potion of Strength, 163
Vodka, vanilla
  Black Mana, 78
  Flavored Enemy, 46
  Never Split the Party Punch, 144
  Power Attack, 64

Whiskey. *See also* Rye whiskey
  about, 15
  Illithid Substance, 104
  1d3 Wandering Minstrels, 106
  Point Blank Shot, 61
  Royal Diplomacy, 65
  Sprite of Hand, 70
  Stunning Smite, 51
  Wight Russian, 113
Whiskey, apple or cinnamon, in Red Mana, 87
Whiskey, peanut butter, in Peanut Butter & Jellikinesis, 95
Whiskey, rye, in Kobold Fashioned, 107
White Mana, 88
Wight Russian, 113
Wine, nonalcoholic mocktail, 176
Wine, sparkling. *See* Champagne or sparkling wine

# About the Authors

**Jon Taylor** is a professional podcaster from San Diego. He has a degree in English Literature from the University of California, Santa Cruz. He spent several years as a stand-up comic on the East Coast before moving back to Southern California. Jon is a cocreator and cohost of the *System Mastery* podcast with Jef, where they review and comment on odd classic RPGs, poking fun at obscure stories and systems while taking the game for a spin. He is one half of the author team for *A Dragon Walks Into a Bar*, *The Ultimate RPG Quest Keeper*, *The Ultimate RPG Tarot Deck*, and *The Düngeonmeister Random Monster Generator*.

**Jef Aldrich** is also a professional podcaster from San Diego. Along with Jon, he has spent the past five years building a podcast brand outside of the big network channels. Jef started entertaining people as a SeaWorld tour guide and eventually just started being funny for a living on his own. Jef is a cocreator and cohost of the *System Mastery* podcast with Jon. He is the other half of the author team for *A Dragon Walks Into a Bar*, *The Ultimate RPG Quest Keeper*, *The Ultimate RPG Tarot Deck*, and *The Düngeonmeister Random Monster Generator*.